What Others are Saying ...

As a father who has lost a daughter, like Paul O'Rear, I know what it's like to live with a broken heart. This book, and the story of Ashley, will take you on an emotional roller coaster ride while dealing with practical issues that everyone who has lost a loved one must face and deal with. It is a testimony as to how adversity can become a valuable teacher to those who are teachable.

—Darrell Scott
Founder, Rachel's Challenge
Author, *Rachel's Tears: The Spiritual Journey of Columbine Martyr Rachel Scott*

Paul has the extraordinary talent to express his loss and his faith that sustains him in stories that speak to the wounded hearts of both mourners and their caregivers, giving them needed hope and support. His insights and stories are enlightening and inspiring for all who struggle after the death of a precious loved one. I consider it a privilege to have Paul as a friend, brother in Christ and fellow mourner. I highly recommend his book for those struggling in grief after the death of a loved one and for those who care for those suffering after the death of a loved one.

—Larry M. Barber, LPC-CS
Certified Thanatologist
Director, GriefWorks, Dallas Texas
Author, *Love Never Dies: Embracing Grief with Hope and Promise*

Paul's book is a blessing for those who have gone down the path no one would ever choose. It is also a gift to those of us who see their pain and suffering. It allows us to believe that parents will go on, with both sadness and eventually, joy.

—Naomi Winick, M.D.
Lowe Foundation Professor in
Pediatric Neuro-Oncology
University of Texas Southwestern
Medical Center

As Paul O'Rear tells of the beautiful life and passing of his daughter, Ashley, the emotions are real and raw. If you've experienced the loss of a loved one, your heart will pound as your emotions are given permission to grieve. Paul reminds us that there is no pre-defined "grieving process" and that no two people grieve alike. As someone who lost three family members within four months, I can say this book is a must read.

—Alene Snodgrass
Author, *Graffiti: Scribbles from
Different Sides of the Street*

Paul O'Rear is a big man with a big heart. In this book, he reaches out with love and compassion to lift up people who are hurting because of the loss of a family member or a child. You will weep and you will rejoice. You will get angry and you will find peace. You will see complete hopelessness turned into unparalleled hope. This book will give you guidance that will strengthen your heart and uplift your soul.

—Dean Kilmer
Senior Advisor for the
Moral Courage Foundation
Author, *Igniting the Moral Courage of America*

Living With a
BROKEN
HEART

Living With a
BROKEN
HEART

Rediscovering Life after Loss

PAUL O'REAR

TATE PUBLISHING
AND ENTERPRISES, LLC

Published by Tate Publishing & Enterprises, LLC
127 E. Trade Center Terrace | Mustang, Oklahoma 73064 USA
1.888.361.9473 | www.tatepublishing.com

Tate Publishing is committed to excellence in the publishing industry. The company reflects the philosophy established by the founders, based on Psalm 68:11,
"The Lord gave the word and great was the company of those who published it."

Book design copyright © 2014 by Tate Publishing, LLC. All rights reserved.
Cover design by Rtor Maghuyop
Interior design by Jake Muelle

Published in the United States of America

ISBN: 978-1-63063-178-9
1. Family & Relationships / Death, Grief, Bereavement
2. Religion / Christian Life / Death, Grief, Bereavement
14.01.02

Dedication

This book is dedicated to the precious memory of my daughter Ashley, who lived more in her fourteen years than most people live in seventy or eighty. It still does not seem real that you are not with us, Ashley. My heart aches beyond belief because of all you had to endure in your short life, but mostly it aches because I cannot hug you and kiss your beautiful little bald head anymore. You are my inspiration for writing this book. Your untimely death has made grief and heartache an inescapable part of my daily life.

But grief and heartache are not the whole story—not even close! You have inspired countless people, including me, with your unwavering courage, your tenacious spirit, and your persistent optimism. You have stolen innumerable hearts, including mine, with your incredibly infectious smile. You have taught me much and inspired me immensely to live every day and to look for all the beauty and all the fun that life has to offer—to *live* with a broken heart. I love you, Ashley, more than you could have possibly imagined while you were confined to an earthly body. I cannot wait to see you again someday, and share together all the incomprehensible beauty that I know you are now experiencing. Until then ...

This book is also dedicated to the sweet memory of my daddy, Larry O'Rear, who taught me what it means to be a man, to be a husband, to be a daddy. You are my hero, Dad, and you always will be. Save a place for me in heaven, because I am coming up to see you one of these days.

And finally, this book is dedicated to the pediatric oncology doctors, nurses, and support staff at Children's Medical Center in Dallas, Texas—and at medical centers and hospitals across the world—who give so much of themselves to bring a little bit of sunshine into the lives of families faced with the darkness of children's cancer.

To those of you who put your heart into your job, who truly care about your patients and their families, who live by the ideal that "we don't treat cancer, we treat children"—thank you! You are a blessing to those of us who must watch our children suffer, as we face the frustration of knowing that we are powerless to make that suffering stop.

You are brave warriors as you battle the cancer monster every day in the children whose lives you touch so profoundly. Sometimes the cancer monster wins, and you go home at night and cry in your pillow. Your heart aches because you know that one more child will not grow up. One more family will walk away from the hospital with broken hearts and empty arms, and it makes you angry that life can be so unfair. Thank you for caring so deeply.

Often the battle is won! The monster is defeated! And one more child *will* grow up to become a mommy or daddy, a teacher or lawyer, a minister or social worker, a business executive or bank president, maybe even a doctor or nurse in a pediatric oncology ward, perhaps even the president of the United States.

With every child whose laughter you restore, this world becomes a better and brighter place. God has entrusted you with the gift of healing through your knowledge and skills and through the wonders of modern medicine, and our lives are greatly enriched by your careful stewardship of that precious gift.

Please do not ever get so discouraged that you quit using your gift, for then the cancer monster will have gained one more step toward victory.

Please understand the importance of what you do. You are our bridge to hope. May God bless you abundantly, as you give so much and bless so many.

—Paul O'Rear
Waxahachie, Texas

Acknowledgements

A very special *thank you* is extended to the following people, whose contributions helped make the publication of this book possible.

Benefactors

Roy and Janice Orr
Brad and Anne Westmoreland
Wes and Pam O'Rear
Dalton and Deanie Taylor
Brian and April Little

Sponsors

Darin and Daena Shelton
"Phil the Great" and Elizabeth Donaldson
Larry and Paula Harms
Daniel and Lacy Hobbs, Grant and Reagan
Tricia Frost
Jerry and Shannon Young
Stephen and Brianne Grove
Troy and Amy Albers
Braxton McMurray

Cheerleaders

My precious wife Susan has always believed in me. She has been by my side "for better or for worse, for richer or poorer (so far it's mostly been poorer!), in sickness and in health, until death do us part," just like she promised all those years ago. She is my soul mate and my biggest cheerleader.

My son Justin is my pride and joy. He has kept me going so many times, without even realizing it, just by being an amazing son and by looking to me for counsel and advice. It is immeasurably good to be considered worthwhile and to be needed by someone so special. In so many ways, I want to be like my son.

My sweet mom, Bettie O'Rear, has always told me what a good writer I am, and has encouraged me to pursue my writing. Here goes, Mom!

Dean Kilmer is a good friend and colleague. He has persistently encouraged me to finish writing this book and get it published so that it can help people. It is due in large part to his incessant nagging that this book now exists. Thank you, Dean!

My brothers—Mark, Wes, David, and Clint—and their beautiful wives and spectacular children, are an integral part of who I am. They are eternally grafted into my soul. Family is everything, and my family can beat up your family any day of the week! Just kidding. They have, however, kept me going and kept me pursuing my writing just by their encouraging words.

I have always felt a special sense of connection and brotherhood with my uncle Tim Bennett. We are a lot alike. We are both loud and obnoxious—him more so than me—and we both find our greatest sense of fulfillment in ministering to others. I look to him as a role model, and have often been renewed in my zeal to be a writer because of my relationship with him.

"Therefore, since we are surrounded by such a great cloud of witnesses, let us throw off everything that hinders and the sin that so easily entangles, and let us run with perseverance the race marked out for us" (Hebrews 12:1 NIV).

My great cloud of witnesses, my cheerleaders from heaven, include: my dad, Larry O'Rear, who was my mentor in life and who will always be my hero; my precious grandparents—Grandpa Horace, Mama Grace, Granddaddy and Grandmama—whose heritage of faith has inspired and blessed me throughout my life; and of course my princess, my Ashley, whose grace and courage continue to amaze and inspire me to be a better person, and whose hugs I miss terribly.

So many other people have lifted me up and cheered me on as I have pursued the sometimes elusive dream of finishing this book. Friends, family, Christian brothers and sisters, coworkers, and sometimes complete strangers to whom I am connected only through electronic relationships via social media, have believed in me and in the value of this project. To them I am indebted and grateful.

This book is for all of you, and for anyone who can be blessed by the message of *Living with a Broken Heart*.

Contents

Ashley with Olympic gold medalist Nikki Stone

Foreword

I always thought the hardest job I'd ever have would be spending a lifetime getting to the Olympics. That is, until I became a parent. Then the Olympics seemed tiny by comparison. As a parent, you haven't only invested your time, energy, strength, and mind—you've also invested your heart. And there are often times your heart is stretched to its very limits because you couldn't imagine caring—or worrying—about anything more. Never was this more apparent to me than when I first met the O'Rears.

It was November 2001 and, as a recent Olympic gold medalist, I was asked to bring an Olympic torch down to a little girl in Texas. She had been selected to carry the flame in the 2002 Olympic torch relay, but the doctors believed she might not make it to her official date. It was only weeks after 9/11 and, like many Americans, I was terrified to get on an airplane. I had boarded the plane bound for Texas and was nearly hyperventilating. I seriously questioned if I should get off the aircraft. Ashley O'Rear was just a name at that point, but there was something powerful compelling me to stay on that plane and meet this young lady and her family.

I didn't know it at the time, but it was truly a decision that changed my life. I not only met an incredibly special little girl with the strength, courage, and passion of a saint, I met a family that would easily go to the ends of the earth for their children. I could tell by the look in Ashley's father's eyes that this sick little girl was his angel. I understood that this was what an invested heart was all about.

The connection with the O'Rears lasted long after I walked out their front door on that impressionable day. Paul has become an inspiration, a role model, and most importantly, a friend. It takes a brave and caring man to share the raw emotions and ultimate lessons learned as a result of the biggest loss most anyone could imagine enduring. I've always been moved at how Paul can reach right into your chest and pull at your heartstrings. Both Paul and his poignant narrative will touch, comfort, and inspire anyone who has been through heartache.

People often marvel at what I handled on one snowy, competitive day in front of the world. Now being a mom, with an invested heart, I know this is nothing compared to what Paul has handled quietly in the small town of Waxahachie, Texas.

—Nikki Stone,
Olympic Gold Medalist
Best-selling Author of *When Turtles Fly*

Introduction

A broken heart. All my life I have heard those words used to describe the emotional fallout a person experiences when life falls apart and comes crashing to the ground.

A junior high boy is brokenhearted when his girlfriend dumps him. How in the world can he go on living after such a devastating loss? Will he ever be able to find true love again? Those questions seem almost amusing when viewed from an adult's perspective. But to that junior high boy, the pain and heartache and uncertainty of life at that moment are no laughing matter.

A little girl's heart breaks when she learns that her precious kitty has run away from home. Two days later her dad discovers that the cat has been run over by a car. That little girl cannot comprehend the thought of kitty being nothing more than a flattened mess of fur and blood and guts in the middle of Main Street. And she certainly cannot bear the pain of never again being able to hold her precious kitty and stroke its soft coat and listen to its gentle purr. How can she go on living with such bitter sorrow in her heart?

A young man's world falls apart when his father dies suddenly and unexpectedly from a rare and fast-growing form of cancer. His hero has fallen. His mentor is gone. The man to whom he was supposed to be able to turn for the answers to life's many challenges is no longer available for that much-needed counsel and advice. Suddenly the abstract concept of a broken heart becomes painfully real.

A young couple's lives are turned upside down when their preteen daughter is diagnosed with a brain tumor. She fights bravely for her life. In time, it looks as though she has beaten the cancer monster. The harsh treatments, which were almost worse than the disease itself, seem to have worked. There appears to be a faint, glimmering light at the end of the long, hellish tunnel through which they have been traveling.

Then, just as their lives are beginning to return to normal, the unthinkable happens. The monster returns, this time much stronger and more determined than before. Within a couple of months their beautiful, bright, precious daughter—now barely a teenager—is stolen from them by death as they stand by and watch helplessly. Never before have their hearts felt this broken, this unmendable. How can such indescribable pain possibly be endured, or even survived?

How Can You Mend a Broken Heart?

Life is not fair. Mom warned us about that harsh reality when we were just kids. In the words of the Shirelles, "Mama said there'd be days like this." Mama was right! Life has a way of knocking you down, throwing you a sucker punch, yanking the rug right out from under your feet. Sometimes you fall so hard that it seems impossible to ever get back up. Often these knock-downs produce an emptiness and a sense of pain that reach to the very core of your being—an emotional state that we often describe as being brokenhearted.

Every one of us will experience these difficult times as we journey through life; times when the heart feels like it is literally broken in two. This brokenness seems to be most intense, and the accompanying emptiness deepest, when someone we love dies.

The question posed musically by the Bee Gees deserves our thoughtful consideration: "How can you mend a broken heart?" Or, even more fundamentally, *can* you mend a broken heart? That is what we will be considering in this book. Particularly, we will explore the concept of grief, and how to survive this gut-wrenching, life-altering experience.

This book is not intended to be a scholarly dissertation on the grief process. I have no credentials in grief counseling and have not done any clinical research into the subject.

I do, however, know grief. I do not just know *about* it. I know it personally and intimately. I have experienced grief on a level so intense that I would not wish such on my worst enemy. I have journeyed into the pit of utter despair, of unspeakable grief…and I have survived.

That is why I have written this book, because I know that grief is survivable. I know that *you* can make it through even the most debilitating heartbreak. My purpose here is simply to share with you my thoughts and my experiences on living with a broken heart, and to give you an encouraging pat on the shoulder and a gentle, reassuring hug as you struggle daily to find your own way through life with your own broken heart.

The Four Cornerstones

When my daughter Ashley died at age fourteen from recurring brain tumors, my world slipped into a tailspin. My heart had never before been so completely broken; life had never before seemed so hopelessly empty. For me and my family, this was virgin territory; these were uncharted waters. Yes, countless people before us had traveled the winding road of grief, but for us this was a new experience.

As we navigated the murky waters that engulfed us on all sides, I realized that there was no roadmap for this journey. Grief grabbed hold of my heart and took me wherever it wanted me to go. There were many days when grief was completely in control, and all I could do was blindly follow its lead.

As the journey unfolded, I found myself surprised at the unpredictable nature of my grief. I had always thought there were certain stages of grief that were common to all grievers, and that these stages were somewhat clinical and even predictable. I had always thought that grief was a process from which the griever "emerged" or "graduated" after a certain amount of time. I had often heard people talk about "closure," and I interpreted that to mean that grief had some definable end point.

I soon learned that many of these preconceptions about grief were completely inaccurate; or at least they were not proving true in my own personal journey. As I struggled to make sense of it all, I discovered some basic truths about grief that caught me by surprise, but that also gave me encouragement and hope. These basic truths provide the philosophical underpinning for this book. They can be thought of as the four cornerstones for *Living with a Broken Heart.*

1. Hearts broken by grief cannot be fixed.

2. Each person grieves in their own way.

3. Grief and Happiness can peacefully coexist.

4. "All things work together for good to those who love God."

The title of this book reflects the reality of the first premise. A heart that is broken by grief simply cannot be fixed. You cannot "get over it and get on with your life." The emptiness does not go away. The pain and heartache do not magically disappear after a prescribed amount of grieving time. "Getting over it" is simply not an option.

You can, however, learn to live *with* a broken heart. You can learn to incorporate that pain and emptiness into your life in some very real and very positive ways. You cannot "get over it," but you certainly *can*—and should—"get on with your life."

My Prayer for You

If you have picked up this book because you have a friend or loved one whose heart is broken, thank you. Brokenhearted people need the love and understanding of gentle, caring people like you. I do not know that I can answer all of your questions about how to help someone grieve, but I will share with you some of my thoughts concerning things that I have found to be helpful.

What I do know is that your simple presence and your genuine love and concern are of far greater value than any words you will speak. Your job is not to help your friend or loved one find healing or overcome their grief. Healing is an elusive process that can only come with time, and even then it is incomplete. There are no "right words" that can be spoken to fix broken hearts because hearts broken by grief cannot be fixed. Your job is simply to love. Sometimes you do not even have to say anything. Just love us and hug us and pray for us, and God will help us figure out the rest.

If you are reading this book because you are in the middle of a broken heart, my prayers are with you. I know something of the road you are traveling. I understand the frustration of other people's expectations concerning your grief. I am well acquainted with the unspeakable pain that arises unbidden in your heart, sometimes with no advance warning and without being specifically provoked. I have experienced the same deep sense of hopelessness that you sometimes find weighing heavily on your soul. There have been times when the heartache has been so intense and the pain so overwhelming, it did not even seem possible that my heart could go on beating within my chest.

My prayer for you is not that your pain will go away, because I believe that such a wish is unrealistic, perhaps even impossible. My prayer is not that God will heal your broken heart, because I am not sure such healing is even attainable. My prayer for you is the same as my prayer for me. I pray that God will grant you peace in the midst of heartache, blessings in the midst of trials, and hope in the midst of despair. I wish you only the best in life, and I hope that you will be able to learn, as I have, to live and to love and to laugh and to enjoy life—*with* a broken heart.

Whatever your reason for reading this book, thank you for assuming that I have something worthwhile to say. I hope I do not let you down.

Ten Years

One final important note, and then we will jump right in. This book was written over a ten-year period. I started writing it shortly after Ashley's death. Within a couple of years, I had about half of it finished. Then I hit a brick wall.

Over the next few years I pulled out the manuscript several times, dusted it off, and made another run at it; but the words simply would not come. During this time I showed my incomplete manuscript to some close friends, and they encouraged me to finish writing the book because its message needed to be heard. So I tried several more times, but it was an exercise in futility. Then in early 2012, a little more than ten years after Ashley's death, I decided it was time to finish this project.

I ended up in the hospital a couple of days before Valentine's Day with a serious infection. While lying in my hospital bed with very little to constructively occupy my time, I pulled out my laptop and started writing.

This time, the words flowed! Within a couple of days, I had written a completely new chapter that was not even in my original outline. Within a few weeks, the book was finished.

I believe the ten-year time frame is significant because the thoughts presented in this book are not all born out of fresh, raw grief. Even the content that was written during those first few months and years has had time to settle and mature. I went back and re-read all of that early content from the vantage point of ten years down the road, and found that it was all still relevant and timely.

I say all of that to say this. The ideas and philosophies presented here have passed the test of time. They are as relevant from the perspective of mature grief as they are from the perspective of fresh, raw grief.

As you read this book, there will be a few places where you will easily discern whether a particular passage was written in the early days, or whether it was written ten years down the road. Beyond that I have intentionally chosen not to separate the earlier writings from the later, or in any other way designate what was written when. I believe this is a valid approach because it honors the timelessness of these principles of grief.

An Angel Gets Her Wings

In the classic movie, *It's A Wonderful Life*, Angel Second Class Clarence Oddbody tells George Bailey that "every time you hear a bell ring, it means that some angel's just got his wings." I did not hear the bells ringing on November 24, 2001, but if Clarence is right then I know they were ringing wildly, because on that cold November day, my own angel Ashley received her wings and flew away to heaven.

Introducing Ashley

Ashley Jean O'Rear was born on April 27, 1987, in Corpus Christi, Texas. I was twenty-five years old, my wife Susan was twenty-two, and Ashley was our first child. We were young, and we were so excited to have been blessed with such a beautiful child.

Ashley was the classic bundle of joy. Her presence in our lives would cause us to experience life, and love, and joy from a whole new perspective and at a much deeper level than we had ever imagined before becoming parents. In the words of a song that I wrote in Ashley's memory shortly after her death:

> The day you came into my life, my world began anew.
> I didn't know that love could run as deep as I love you.

Probably the most characteristic quality that became apparent very early in Ashley's life was her upbeat, positive, happy attitude. My heart is filled with priceless memories of the fourteen years we had with Ashley, and our house is filled with photographs that preserve those memories and make them more tangible. Rare is the picture in which she is not smiling or laughing.

Even in those snapshots that encapsulate only a split second of time, there is an infectious enthusiasm in her eyes and in her smile that reaches out and grabs you and will not let go. There was something almost magical about her spirit that stole the hearts of nearly everyone who knew her. I miss that magic.

Though her personality was quite animated, she was not very excitable. I remember one particular occasion when Ashley was about three or four years old. Susan and I were sitting in the living room watching television, and Ashley and Justin were in their rooms playing. From Ashley's room came a wee, distant voice, "Daaaaddy, I stuck."

Susan and I got up from the couch and proceeded to Ashley's room. We entered the doorway but did not see Ashley anywhere. Once again I heard the voice, "Daaaaddy, I stuck." Following her voice, we found Ashley on the floor, her head wedged between the bed and the wall. She could not move and was unable to free herself, but she did not panic or become hysterical. Nor was she crying or screaming, which would have been the expected reaction from any typical three or four-year-old child. Rather, she simply called for help in a very calm voice, and Daddy came and rescued her.

I like that phrase, "rescued her," because it conjures up the image of a knight in shining armor coming to the rescue of his princess. Every daddy wants to think that he is his little girl's hero. For me, there will be no more opportunities to be Ashley's hero, so I must hold dearly the memories of occasions such as the one just described. As silly as it may seem, doing so helps me cling to a hope that perhaps I fulfilled the role of hero for my precious little girl.

School Days

In the fall of 1996, Ashley entered her fourth grade year at T. C. Wilemon Elementary School in Waxahachie, Texas. Wilemon was a wonderful old school that had begun its existence many years earlier as a high school, then served as a junior high school, and was now one of Waxahachie's five elementary schools.

There was something magical about Wilemon Elementary. The building was old and dilapidated and in serious need of repair. The gymnasium was hot in the summer and cold in the winter, and though it was the only facility suitable for school programs and assemblies, the acoustics were horrible. In spite of these challenges, the people of Wilemon made it a truly magical place.

The school's principal, Mrs. O'Daniel, loved the kids and they knew it. The teachers were outstanding, and everyone seemed to care genuinely, deeply, and personally about making sure their students received the best educational experience possible. There was a noticeable sense of family among the staff, and this special bond enveloped the students and their families as well.

Even the facility itself, though old and worn out, contributed to the sense of magic. The front lawn was shaded by majestic old trees that towered high above even the tallest "big person." A grand, impressive set of cement steps led up to the ornate main entrance to the school, located on the second of three floors. Walking the halls, it was impossible to miss the overwhelming sense that this magnificent old building had nurtured thousands upon thousands of young, impressionable minds through the years, standing guard over them in their pursuit of knowledge.

Never before or since have we been a part of anything quite like the Wilemon experience. Even as I write these words, I am overcome by a sense of nostalgia, and I long to be able to return to those simple days when my kids were part of the Wilemon family.

Troubling Symptoms

Sometime in January or February of 1997, shortly after Wilemon Elementary students returned from Christmas break, Ashley began waking up in the mornings feeling nauseated. Often she would throw up, and then she would feel better and go on to school. She was having sinus and allergy problems at the same time, and we just figured the nausea and vomiting were the result of sinus drainage building up in her stomach overnight. We began seeking a remedy with over-the-counter allergy and sinus medications.

On a few occasions Ashley got sick and vomited while at school. We still were not terribly concerned, because there had been a number of viruses and other bugs going around among the students, and we just figured she had picked up something contagious from a classmate.

In March of that year, I led a church ski trip to Loveland Ski Area in Colorado. Susan and the kids went with me. Ashley had been feeling better for several days prior to our departure, and we were encouraged by that. Upon arriving in Colorado, however, the nausea and vomiting returned. We were at a much higher elevation than that to which we were accustomed, and high elevations can sometimes result in altitude sickness, which can manifest itself in various symptoms including nausea and vomiting. So, once again, there seemed to be a logical explanation for Ashley's ailments.

We arrived in Colorado on Monday afternoon, and skied on Tuesday, Wednesday, and Thursday. On Thursday, Ashley threw up seven times while skiing. We were beginning to grow more concerned. Susan and I left one of the other adult chaperones in charge at the ski area and took Ashley to a clinic in a nearby town. The doctor examined Ashley and performed some tests, one of which was a urinalysis. The urinalysis revealed a serious bladder infection. Ashley was put on a strong antibiotic to fight the infection, and Phenergan was prescribed to help with the nausea and vomiting.

We were relieved. Finally, it seemed, we had discovered the cause of the problems that had been plaguing Ashley for a couple of months. Finally, it seemed, we had turned the corner and had a specific plan of attack to get the problems under control. Finally, it seemed, relief was in sight.

That night after returning to the ski area, Ashley was up and down several times throughout the night feeling nauseated and vomiting. It was an extremely unpleasant night. The next morning we loaded up everything and everyone and began the twenty hour trek back home to Texas. Ashley slept much of the way. When she was awake, however, she was complaining of double vision. That concerned us; but again, we thought we had already discovered the cause of her ailments; and again, sudden changes in altitude can cause some unusual symptoms to appear temporarily.

We arrived back home in Waxahachie in the wee hours of Saturday morning. After a good night's sleep in our own beds, Saturday was kind of a lazy day. We ran a few errands and spent most of the day at home. Saturday evening we rented a movie to enjoy watching together as a family. During the movie, Ashley suddenly began complaining once again about her vision. Susan and I grew more concerned.

Seeking Answers

I called a friend of ours, Mike, who is an eye doctor. I explained briefly about Ashley's sudden double vision during the trip home from Colorado and asked if he could look at her. He invited us to bring Ashley over to his house.

When we arrived at Mike's house, he brought out a small flashlight and began testing Ashley's eyes. He also looked into her eyes with some of his instruments. After examining her, Mike told us that he was a little concerned. There were a couple of things that he had observed in Ashley's eyes that he said are usually not found in combination. He also said that, for Ashley to have suddenly started experiencing double vision, there had to be something that was causing the double vision. We needed to find out what that something was.

Mike recommended that we take Ashley to Children's Medical Center in Dallas, about forty minutes away, to have a CT scan performed in order to pinpoint the problem. He called ahead to Children's and told them we were coming. We quickly made arrangements for someone to watch our son Justin, and then headed to Dallas. It was about 10:30 p.m.

On the trip to Dallas, numerous thoughts were running through my mind. *What could possibly be causing Ashley's double vision? Could it still just be lingering side effects of high altitude sickness? We do not even have insurance for Ashley. What if we get there and they turn us away because of our lack of insurance coverage? Are we over-reacting? Is this just really no big deal, and here we are rushing to a children's specialty hospital in Dallas late at night like it is some life-threatening emergency?*

Before I knew it, we were pulling up to the emergency room entrance. My stomach was churning.

I was worried about Ashley, I was worried about the whole insurance thing, and I was a little uneasy taking my only daughter into a hospital that I knew nothing about and just turning her over to them. I parked the car and we took Ashley inside.

After explaining our situation to the triage nurse and filling out some preliminary paperwork, Ashley was put into an examination room and a CT scan was ordered. It was now about midnight. An hour passed. Then an hour and a half. Doctors and nurses came into the room periodically to ask questions and examine Ashley. Finally, the CT scan machine became available. Ashley was taken to the scan room in a wheelchair.

After Ashley was put onto the moveable table that would be used to slide her under the massive CT scan machine, Susan and I were escorted into an observation room where we could watch as the scan was performed. The testing began, and we could see images of Ashley's brain as they appeared on the monitors in front of the CT technician.

Our World Collapses

At 2:30 a.m., a doctor came into the observation room and asked Susan and me to step out into the hallway with him. He escorted us down the hall a short distance to a cubbyhole with some chairs and asked us to sit down. The words he spoke next changed our lives forever. "Your daughter has a brain tumor."

I was stunned. Surely I had not heard him correctly. I do not even remember anything else the doctor said.

After he left, Susan and I sat there for a few minutes trying to comprehend what we had just been told. Susan made the comment that this was all just like a bad dream. It seemed so unreal.

We both broke down and cried. We promised each other right then and there that, no matter what happened, we would not let anything tear us apart. We were in this together. We would do everything within our power to make sure Ashley had the best possible chance of surviving. She was only nine-years old— almost ten—and had her whole life ahead of her.

The rest of that morning is a blur. Ashley was admitted to the hospital and was eventually moved to a regular room. After she had settled in, I drove the thirty-five miles back home to Waxahachie to begin the task of informing our family and friends of Ashley's condition.

That was the longest thirty-five miles I have ever driven. I prayed like I had never prayed before in my life. I cried like I had never cried before in my life. I begged God to spare my precious little girl's life, to heal her, to make the tumor miraculously disappear as though it had never even been there, or to at least use the doctors and nurses to successfully remove all traces of the tumor and allow Ashley a full and complete recovery. I was scared, like I had never been scared before in my life.

I arrived home at about 6:30 on Sunday morning. I picked up the phone and called Susan's family and my family to share with them the grave news. I called a few other people at churches we had been associated with in the past, and at our current church, and asked them to begin praying fervently for Ashley.

Then I sat down at my computer and composed an e-mail with the subject line, "Urgent Prayer Request." In it I briefly explained Ashley's condition, and asked the recipients of the e-mail to begin praying fervently for Ashley. I also requested that the message be forwarded to as many people as possible, as quickly as possible.

That simple little e-mail, sent to a total of twenty-six people, ended up being forwarded all over the world. As a result, thousands upon thousands of people offered up prayers for Ashley and for our family. We received countless well-wishes in the form of e-mails, cards, and gifts from family and friends, as well as from complete strangers. Our lives were richly blessed and deeply touched by such an outpouring of love.

First Steps

On Tuesday, March 18, beginning about 9:30 a.m., Ashley underwent brain surgery for the purpose of removing the golf-ball-sized tumor that had been discovered two days earlier. At 3:30 p.m., the pediatric neurosurgeon, Dr. Swift, came out into the waiting room to tell us the results of the six-hour operation.

He was able to remove about ninety-five percent of the tumor. The entire tumor could not be removed because it was attached to the brain stem. Dr. Swift did not want to risk damage to the brain stem, which could have resulted in extremely severe neurological trauma. Therefore, an estimated five percent of the mass was left in Ashley's brain. Ashley spent a couple of days in intensive care following surgery and then was moved to a regular room.

Six days after surgery, the oncologists met with us briefly to let us know that Ashley's pathology report showed her brain tumor to be cancerous. Technically, it was classified as a medulloblastoma, "a fast-growing, invasive tumor which frequently metastasizes to other parts of the central nervous system via the spinal fluid".[1] The good news was that "this tumor is very responsive to treatment with surgery, radiation and chemotherapy".[2]

Ashley underwent minor surgery the next day to implant a portacath[3] just under the skin in her chest. The portacath would be used as an access point for her upcoming chemotherapy treatments.

Ashley's recovery from brain surgery was impressive, though there were some lingering deficits—and even some permanent deficits—suffered as a result of the surgery. Ashley had been right-handed prior to surgery. Because she was left with a severe deficit in her fine motor skills and in coordination on her right side, Ashley taught herself to write—and to do just about everything—left-handed. Even later as her right-side motor skills and strength began to improve, she continued to favor using her left hand for most tasks.

The Plan

The day after Ashley's portacath surgery, the oncologists sat down with us again, this time to present the plan that had been devised for Ashley's treatments. We were not prepared for what we were about to hear.

The protocol under which she would be treated was relatively new and called for a combination of radiation therapy and chemotherapy. The radiation therapy would take place once each day, five days per week, for six weeks. Each session would take about an hour to an hour and a half.

In addition to radiation, four very powerful cancer-fighting drugs would be introduced into Ashley's body on a rotating basis. Each cycle would take six weeks, and there would be a total of eight cycles. That meant we were looking at more than a year's worth of treatments between the radiation and the chemotherapy. We were completely overwhelmed!

Everyone knows that cancer treatments can have some severe side effects. It has been said that, with cancer, sometimes the treatment is worse than the disease. We learned the bitter truth of that statement as we watched our precious little girl suffer through what ended up being almost a year and a half of hell.

We were told that, as a result of radiation and chemotherapy, Ashley would lose all of her beautiful blonde hair, and would probably experience extensive nausea and vomiting from time to time. Other side effects, with varying degrees of severity, were possible as well. She would be required to be hospitalized for five days every six weeks while receiving one of the four drugs, because that particular drug had some dangerous potential side effects and would require close monitoring during treatment.

The Lighter Side

By the time we were able to bring Ashley home from her initial hospital stay, she had been in the hospital for nearly two weeks. During that time she received visits from family, friends, church members, teachers, classmates, and even total strangers. As cards, banners, and letters came in, we began to hang them around the room until every wall of her hospital room was covered with get-well wishes. The stuffed animals, toys, flowers, and other gifts were stacked in every conceivable nook and cranny, and balloons were tied in bunches all around the room.

As we were leaving the hospital, the man at the front desk asked me for the last name of the patient. I said, "O'Rear." He responded, "Oh, Ashley. Our phone calls will be cut in half now that she is leaving!" On subsequent hospital visits we would develop a very special bond with this man, Ron, who we came to know as "Grumpaw." He was always very kind to Ashley, and we grew to love him dearly.

The lady at the admitting desk commented, "She has been a popular little girl while she was here!" One man who had been working at the hospital for about four years said that he had never seen a patient who had received as many phone calls, visitors, and gifts as Ashley.

What a wonderful blessing it is to have so many people who care so deeply, and who are willing to express their love so tangibly.

The Journey Begins

Less than a week after Ashley left the hospital, the long and arduous journey down the path to healing had its beginning. We took Ashley to St. Paul hospital in Dallas, just down the road from Children's Medical Center, to begin the radiation treatments. We would get a taste very early of how treacherous the journey would be.

When the day for her first treatments arrived, we took Ashley to Children's to get her very first chemotherapy injection. After the injection, we took her down the street to St. Paul to receive her first radiation treatment. She did fine through both the chemotherapy and radiation treatments.

After radiation, we drove across Dallas to a place that specializes in wigs for cancer patients. Ashley tried several wigs and picked one that she liked, very similar in color and length to her own hair. Then we started for home.

At about 1:30 p.m., while traveling down North Central Expressway in Dallas, Ashley suddenly began to feel nauseated. Fortunately, we had brought a "throw-up bucket" with us. Ashley began vomiting, and vomited all the way home.

We arrived home and got her into the house and situated on the couch. She continued vomiting. We called Children's and spoke to one of Ashley's nurses and explained what was going on. She called in a prescription to our pharmacy for some Phenergan suppositories. I rushed to the pharmacy, picked up the medicine, came back home, and administered the medicine to Ashley. The Phenergan calmed Ashley's nausea and put an end to the vomiting, allowing Ashley to rest. By the time it was over, she had vomited almost continuously for about two hours.

Friday morning we woke up, gave Ashley an oral dose of Phenergan elixir, then headed to St. Paul for her second radiation treatment, hoping the aftereffects would not be a repeat of the day before. Ashley was difficult to awaken, and then she slept in the car all the way to the hospital. This did not really surprise us since she had experienced such a rough day on Thursday, and Phenergan tends to make one drowsy as well.

We arrived at St. Paul early and took Ashley inside. She continued to sleep until the nurse came out into the waiting room to get us. Susan and I both followed Ashley and the nurse into the treatment room to help get Ashley ready for her treatment. While the nurse was helping Ashley climb up onto the radiation table, Ashley bent over at the waist and fell forward onto the table. Thinking she was just really tired and wanted to lie down, I leaned over to ask her if that was the case. She responded in a very sleepy voice. As the nurse was helping Ashley stand back up, Ashley passed out in her arms. We quickly found a sheet, spread it out on the floor, and laid Ashley down. The nurse called for assistance.

Ashley was only "out" for a few seconds before waking up. The radiation oncologist called off her treatment for that day and sent us back over to Children's. They did a CT scan to see if there were any fluid collections, blockages, or areas of pressure build-up in Ashley's brain. The scan came back showing none of these problems, for which we were very thankful.

The doctors then considered the possibility that Ashley had experienced a seizure, but quickly ruled out that as well. The best they could figure, Ashley was still weak from Thursday's vomiting spell and had not replenished her fluids back to adequate levels. Added to that were the effects of the Phenergan making her sleepy and consequently weak, and it was just too much for her little body to deal with, causing her to faint. After spending most of the day at Children's, we headed back home to Waxahachie. We were looking forward to a peaceful weekend with no trips to Dallas.

On Monday morning, we made the trek back to St. Paul and Ashley received her second radiation treatment. After the treatment, we stopped back by Children's to visit with the nurses and ask some questions. While we were waiting to see the nurses, Ashley began feeling nauseated and started throwing up again. Once again, the vomiting spell lasted for about two hours before it subsided. It was horrible. There was nothing we could do but sit by and stroke her forehead as we watched her little body convulse in agony. I guess the good thing about this attack was that it happened at the hospital, so the doctors and nurses saw exactly what she was experiencing.

When it became obvious that the vomiting was not going to stop, Ashley was put in a room and given a couple of medicines by injection. She was then put on intravenous fluids to re-hydrate her and was given another medicine or two through the IV. The doctor decided to admit Ashley to the hospital so that she could be monitored overnight and could continue receiving IV fluids to rebuild her strength. She was also given several anti-nausea and antacid medicines to prepare her little tummy for Tuesday's radiation treatment.

On Tuesday morning, I took Justin to school and then headed back to Dallas for Ashley's radiation treatment. I arrived at Children's just before Ashley was to be transported over to St. Paul. She really looked good, and Susan said that she had slept well throughout the night.

We went to St. Paul and Ashley had her radiation treatment without any problems. After radiation, we returned to Children's to sit for a few hours, just in case she had another severe reaction to the radiation. We watched her closely for any signs of an upset tummy or nausea.

We had decided that 1:30 p.m. would be our benchmark, because that was when she had started vomiting after her first radiation treatment. As we watched the clock with nervous anticipation, one thirty came and went without any problems, so we asked to be discharged. We were given prescriptions for the medications Ashley had received through her IV so that we could continue administering them in pill form. After all the discharge paperwork was finished, we finally left Children's sometime around 3:00 or 4:00 p.m. and headed home. We now had one good day behind us, and that felt pretty good!

The Long and Winding Road

The forty-eight-week protocol of chemotherapy stretched into almost a year and a half due to complications along the way. On one occasion Ashley's portacath became irreparably clogged, and she had to have it removed and another one surgically implanted on the other side of her chest before treatments could be resumed.

At another point, she quit eating. She wanted to eat, but for some reason she simply could not. We didn't understand it, the doctors didn't understand it, and even Ashley didn't understand it. As the doctors tried to remedy this situation, Ashley's weight dropped from seventy-five pounds to fifty-eight pounds. For a period of time, malnourishment was as big a concern as the cancer. As a last resort, the doctors surgically implanted a rubber feeding tube through Ashley's stomach wall and directly into her stomach. This tube was used for daily feedings until she was able to start eating again on her own. The feeding tube literally saved her life.

Many other complications arose along the way. Routine hospital stays quite often turned into lengthy hospital stays. Unplanned, late-night trips to the hospital due to a sudden fever were not uncommon. Low blood counts resulted in the need for blood transfusions. Infections temporarily derailed the treatment protocol. Everyday plans had to be shuffled and rearranged at the last minute due to some unexpected complication. Weakness and nausea and vomiting and pain became a normal part of daily life.

Cancer and the treatments used to combat it are a nightmare that I would not wish on anyone. I cannot even describe the gut-wrenching horror of watching your child writhe in agony, knowing that there is absolutely nothing you can do to make it stop. I cannot make you understand, unless you have experienced it yourself, the complete sense of helplessness and despair that overwhelms a parent's soul at such a time. I would have traded places with Ashley in a heartbeat to spare her the unspeakable torment she experienced, but I could not spare her. Through it all, however, she exhibited a graceful spirit and a tenacious courage such as I have never seen even in the most mature adult.

I am still amazed when I think back on everything she went through, and her remarkable attitude toward it all. She despised the idea of anyone feeling sorry for her or taking pity on her. On one occasion, when someone announced in church that she was sick, she looked up at Susan and said rather matter-of-factly, "I'm not sick! I just have a brain tumor."

She never used her cancer as an excuse to slack off in school. Instead, she worked harder and studied longer than probably any other student to keep up her grades. She would even get upset with Susan and me when we would make her stop working on her homework at one or two o'clock in the morning so that she could get some sleep. She was determined to get her work done, and her grades were evidence of her determination. Throughout her entire treatment protocol, she maintained an A average in every one of her classes! *That's my girl!*

Ashley never understood the fact that she was an inspiration to so many people. In her mind, she was just a normal kid who had to face a few struggles in life. The only thing that made sense to her was to just keep going, to not let the cancer slow her down, and to enjoy everything about life. It was those very qualities that in fact did inspire others—and still continue to inspire others—to face life's struggles with courage and determination. She did not consider herself extraordinary in any way; and that is one of the things that actually made her extraordinary.

The Rest of the Story

As the date for Ashley's last chemotherapy treatment approached, we began to plan a No More Chemo party. Many friends and family members came to help us celebrate. Ashley had emerged from her cancer journey alive, and she was ready to tackle whatever life had in store for her.

She began making plans for the future. Because of what she had been through, and inspired by some of the wonderfully caring healthcare professionals who had made her journey more bearable, Ashley decided she wanted to be a child life specialist when she grew up. She wanted to be able to help other children who were suffering through various diseases and traumatic health issues, in the same way that Lesley, Ashley's child life specialist at Children's, had been such a tremendous help to her. She really felt like she had found her calling, and she was excited about the future.

For three years, every MRI and CT scan came back clean. There was no sign of cancer. Every indication pointed to the fact that Ashley was cancer-free! Dr. Winick, the beautiful soul who had served as Ashley's primary oncologist throughout her entire cancer ordeal, later told us that she had taken Ashley off of her worry list.

Then came September 11, 2001. We heard the news reports of the planes crashing into the World Trade Center towers on our car radio as we traveled from Waxahachie to Children's Medical Center in Dallas. Ashley had begun exhibiting some troubling signs over the previous few weeks, and the doctors wanted to do a CT scan and possibly an MRI to see what might be causing those symptoms.

That day will be forever etched in my memory. The tragic events that we watched unfold throughout the day on the hospital's television sets were unimaginable. As we would learn early the next morning, our own unimaginable tragedy was about to unfold as well.

On the morning of September 12, we received a phone call from one of the doctors at Children's Medical Center. He had examined Ashley's scans from the day before, and there were some new spots that had not been present on her previous MRI. Ashley's cancer was back.

Once again she faced her opponent with courage and tenacity. Once again she was determined that the cancer would not win. Once again she maintained a graceful spirit in the face of incredible obstacles. The only difference was, this time the cancer was stronger.

This time it grew faster. This time it refused to be defeated. On Saturday afternoon, November 24, 2001, Ashley's struggle ended. She died at home in our bed, surrounded by family and friends who loved her more than words can express. She slipped from this life peacefully, and went home to be with Jesus. She was fourteen years old.

Life is not the same without her. Life will never be the same without her. I learned so much about life, about love, about faith, and about hope by watching my princess struggle courageously and with incredible grace as she faced, literally, the battle of her life. Our lives are better because she was here. There is something missing in our lives because she is gone.

> Her absence hurts so much
> because her presence brought so much joy.

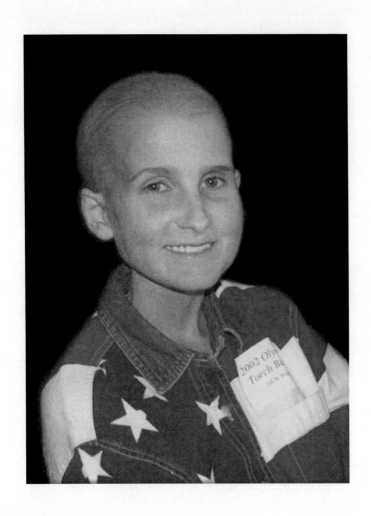

Ashley's Legacy

A shley turned fourteen in April 2001. She had spent the previous four years of her life battling cancer and all the demons that come with it, including the cruel side effects of the very medicines and treatments that were designed to save her life. Even three years after her final chemotherapy treatment, there were still some very frustrating long-term side effects that she had to deal with every day.

Through it all, she seldom complained. She had developed a courage that would serve any warrior well; a determination that would see the fiercest athlete through the most difficult challenge; and an indomitable spirit that exemplified the motto—"Never give up."

Because of these qualities, and because of the thousands of people who followed Ashley's story through my Internet and e-mail updates, Ashley became an inspiration to people all over the world. People found the courage to face their own life struggles because of the inspiration they gained from Ashley's story.

Trust in God

Sometime during the spring surrounding her fourteenth birthday, I learned that the Salt Lake Organizing Committee for the 2002 Olympic Winter Games was accepting nominations for Olympic torchbearers. The motto for the 2002 winter games was "Light the Fire Within," and the torchbearers' theme was "Inspire." The organizing committee wanted to showcase the stories of people who inspired others, by inviting them to be torchbearers. So they asked America to nominate people who were worthy of such an honor.

Naturally, Ashley was the first person who came to my mind. I sent the following essay to the Salt Lake Organizing Committee, telling Ashley's inspirational story in 100 words or less:

> Ashley is my daughter. At age 9 she was diagnosed with a brain tumor. She underwent brain surgery followed by radiation and chemotherapy for 1-1/2 years. Today she is 14 and a survivor. The story of her courageous battle with cancer and her determination to beat this disease has inspired countless people who followed her story via the Internet, some of whom were engaged in their own cancer battle. She still struggles with some residual side effects of the treatments, but she continues to face her struggles with courage and determination.

On July 11, 2001, I opened my e-mail and found the following message from Mitt Romney, President and CEO of the Salt Lake Organizing Committee. The subject line read, "Congratulations! You have been selected as an Olympic torchbearer."

> Dear Ashley O'Rear,
>   For the last two months, community judging panels across America have been reading tens

of thousands of stories, submitted by people from all walks of life who want to honor someone who has been a source of personal inspiration in their lives. The panels' task has been to choose a few special people who are the light of inspiration in our nation to serve as torchbearers for the Salt Lake 2002 Olympic torch relay.

On behalf of the Salt Lake Organizing Committee for the 2002 Olympic Winter Games, and our presenting sponsors Coca-Cola and Chevrolet, it is my privilege to inform you that you have been selected by our judges as a potential torchbearer to be honored in the Olympic torch relay. I would personally like to invite you to help carry the Olympic flame as it travels across America. Congratulations!

I read the e-mail three or four times, just to make sure I had not misinterpreted something or that my eyes were not playing tricks on me. Then I shared the exciting news with Ashley: she was going to carry the Olympic torch!

The e-mail went on to say that an official public announcement revealing the names of all torchbearers would not be made until late August. We were asked to keep the news within our immediate family until after the official announcement had been made. We anxiously awaited the organizing committee's announcement, so that we could start telling everyone we knew!

On Thursday, October 18, 2001, the mayor of Dallas, Texas—Ron Kirk—held a press conference at Dallas City Hall to officially announce the passing of the Olympic flame through the city of Dallas on December 12. Ashley was one of over one hundred torchbearers from the Dallas/Fort Worth area who were present for the press conference.

Susan said that the whole time Mayor Kirk was talking he kept looking at Ashley, who was sitting in her wheelchair on the front row wearing a bold, bright, patriotic flag shirt. Three torchbearers had been invited to briefly tell the story of how they were nominated to carry the Olympic flame. The final speaker was unable to attend the press conference, so Mayor Kirk asked Ashley if she would like to come up and say a few words. Ashley's voice was too weak to be heard in such a large crowd, so I wheeled her up to the front of the room and proceeded to tell her story:

> Ashley is fourteen years old. When she was just about to turn ten, we found out that she had a brain tumor. We spent a lot of days and nights at Children's Medical Center in Dallas. She fought it bravely. She overcame it. She was in remission for about four years. It was during that time that I nominated her [to carry the Olympic torch], because of the courage that she had shown and the inspiration that she had been to so many people all over the world. We got the letter saying that she had been invited to participate [in the torch relay].
>
> Then, just about a month ago, we found out that her tumors were back. So we're fighting the battle once again. To me, that just adds a whole new level of meaning to realize that here she is fighting again, and she is going to be

representing the very best of the human spirit as she carries the Olympic flame through the Dallas/Fort Worth area.

As I wheeled Ashley away from the podium to once again take our place in the crowd, the whole room erupted in spontaneous applause and rousing cheers for Ashley. Once again, her spirit and her courage had touched the hearts of complete strangers.

After the press conference had concluded, several news crews came up to Ashley and asked if they could interview her. One reporter asked her, "What would you say to the people of New York who experienced such a devastating tragedy on September eleven?"

Ashley's answer to that question was at the same time beautifully simple and deeply profound. It revealed a genuine faith and trust in God that I strive to emulate every day of my life.

Here was a fourteen-year-old girl whose body had been completely ravaged by the hideous monster we call cancer. She was too weak to stand and walk without assistance. She required the use of a wheelchair—and someone to push the wheelchair—just to get where she wanted to go. She had suffered more physical pain in her short life than most people will ever experience. So many things had been stolen from her by this monster: her beautiful hair, her physical strength, her independence. No child should have to endure the monumental trials that she had experienced in her short life.

Yet without a moment's hesitation, she quietly and thoughtfully answered the reporter's question.

"What would you say to the people of New York who experienced such a devastating tragedy on September eleven?" Here is her answer.

> Keep believing in God, that He can help; that
> if you believe and just keep relying on Him, He
> will help you make it through all your troubles.

I have spent almost all of my adult life serving as a minister, and I still struggle sometimes to have a faith that is so genuine, so simple, and so completely trusting.

Never Give Up

It was Tuesday morning, April 11, 2000. The peaceful silence of restful sleep was broken by the ringing of the telephone at 5:00 a.m. I answered the phone to hear the voice of Kidd Kraddick, the host of the *Kidd Kraddick in the Morning* radio show that originates on Dallas/Fort Worth radio station 106.1 KISS FM and is syndicated across the country.

Kidd and his co-hosts—Kellie Rasberry and Big Al Mack—were going to be serving as celebrity escorts later that day at the annual Beyond the Rainbow Luncheon and Fashion Show hosted by Children's Cancer Fund of Dallas. This gala event draws thousands of the Dallas/Fort Worth area's business executives, socialites, professional athletes, and celebrities each year to raise money for life-saving research and treatment programs that will lead to a cure for childhood cancer. Ashley had served as a calendar artist and fashion model for

Beyond the Rainbow in 1998, and then as a friendship model in 1999.

The night before the 5:00 a.m. phone call, Kidd Kraddick had been searching the Internet, looking for information about Children's Cancer Fund and Beyond the Rainbow to prepare for his participation that next morning, and to be able to discuss the fundraising event on his show prior to attending the luncheon. In his search, he came across a guest editorial that I had submitted to our local newspaper, the Waxahachie Daily Light, a few years prior. It was entitled, "Choose to be Happy," and is reprinted in a later chapter of this book, also entitled "Choose to be Happy."

In that newspaper piece, Kidd learned about Ashley and her cancer battle. That prompted him to do some additional searching to see if he could find any updated information about Ashley's condition. The most current information he found was my Internet update which I had posted in September 1999, some six months prior. Kidd found himself engrossed in Ashley's story and eager to find out how she was doing at that time. So he looked up our phone number and called us at 5:00 a.m.

He asked how Ashley was doing, and I updated him on her status. After we chatted for a few minutes, he asked if it would be okay for him to conduct live interviews with both me and Ashley, by telephone, on his morning radio show in a couple of hours. I woke Ashley up, explained about the phone call, told her that Kidd Kraddick wanted to interview her on the radio, and asked her if that would be okay. I was not at all surprised at her answer. "Yes! That will be okay!"

The on-air interview lasted about sixteen minutes. Kidd, Kellie, and Big Al were all very gracious in their comments and questions to Ashley and me. Near the end of Kidd's interview with Ashley he said, "Hey, Ashley, I'm going to ask you a really, really hard question, okay? If somebody else finds out in the next week or so— somebody your age—that they have cancer, that they have a brain tumor, what advice would you give them to help them get through it?"

Once again, Ashley's answer was at the same time beautifully simple and deeply profound. It revealed an unconquerable spirit.

Here was a thirteen-year-old girl who had been knocked down so many times she could have easily, and understandably, just thrown in the towel. Who would have blamed her for saying, "I give up"? Even in her apparent victory over cancer, the battle had certainly taken its toll. There were challenges that she faced every day. Even simple, everyday tasks were more difficult. Here is an excerpt from my September 1999 update.

> The worst part of junior high, so far, has been the homework. Ashley has been staying up until midnight or later, just about every night, in order to get her homework finished.
>
> The most dramatic performance-related effect we are seeing as a result of the treatments (and probably specifically as a result of the radiation), is that it takes Ashley much longer to accomplish most tasks. When we sit down as a family to eat, Ashley is always the last one to finish her meal. Walking is still a slower process

than it used to be. She still writes left-handed, which she taught herself to do when the brain tumor surgery left her with severely diminished fine motor skills on her right side.

Whether these losses are permanent or temporary, only time will tell.

Did Ashley use her medical condition as an excuse to lower her expectations of herself? No. Instead, she just pushed herself harder and kept at it longer to make sure she got all her homework finished and turned in, and to make sure she kept her grades up. She often even refused the modifications to her school assignments that she was allowed by law that would have lightened her load. She just kept pushing forward, no matter the challenge.

So, when this thirteen-year-old, never-say-die warrior was asked by a radio celebrity—whom she happened to idolize—what advice she would give to another kid who was given a cancer diagnosis, her answer was not hollow. It was not simply some philosophical ideal that she had read somewhere or seen in a movie. Her answer came from deep in the trenches of her own daily experience. This was her own battle-tested philosophy of life that had seen her through the darkest of days.

"If somebody your age finds out in the next week or so that they have a brain tumor, what advice would you give them to help them get through it?"

Her quiet, timid reply was almost imperceptible over the radio, but it carried all the force and authority of a grizzly bear standing upright and roaring at the top of its lungs.

> To stay happy and not feel bad about themselves.
> Pray. Never give up.

Learning from Ashley

Trust in God, and never give up. This is Ashley's Legacy. It was the battle cry by which she fought her own battle, and it is the heroic advice that she timidly offered whenever she was asked how to make it through life's darkest days.

In facing the deep despair and utter emptiness of losing Ashley at such a young age, we have simply taken a page from her playbook as *we* struggle to make it through life's darkest days: "Trust in God, and never give up."

Bettie and Larry O'Rear on their honeymoon, July 1956

Get Over It?

A Love Story

Larry was twenty-three years old when he moved to the small south Texas town of Alice. He had graduated from Abilene Christian College a couple of years earlier, had spent some time preaching and trying to sell insurance, and now was settling into a new job in a new town teaching math and science courses at William Adams High School.

He was tall, dark, and handsome—and single—and happened to catch the eye of a young sixteen-year-old girl named Bettie who was a student at William Adams High School. Bettie's father was an elder at the local Church of Christ where Larry began attending.

A certain chemistry began to develop between this young man who taught that very subject, and the high school girl whose heart he was in the process of unwittingly stealing. The two began dating secretly, so as not to raise eyebrows. After all, he was a teacher and she was a student! On Sundays after church, they would sometimes drive to Mathis Lake about thirty miles away and spend lazy afternoons just talking and holding hands and enjoying each other's company, usually still dressed in their Sunday church clothes. Often they would be accompanied by Bettie's best friend and her beau.

The following summer, Larry made a trip to New Mexico where he spent several weeks participating in a Physics Institute sponsored by the University of New Mexico at Albuquerque. He and Bettie wrote to each other almost every day while they were apart. Romance was beginning to blossom into a full and beautiful flower.

Larry returned from New Mexico and began his second year of teaching at the high school. Bettie was now a senior. In December of that year, Larry asked Bettie if she wanted to cook and keep house for him. "That was just the kind of romantic that he was," Bettie recalled years later. "And, idiot that I was, I said 'Yes!'" Bettie graduated from William Adams High School in May of 1956, and on July 27 of that same year she and Larry were married.

Larry and Bettie are my parents. Over the course of thirty-three years of marriage, Mom and Dad shared countless joys and numerous heartaches. They shared the immense joy of bringing five children into the world and watching them grow into young men. They experienced financial ups and downs. They shared the deep heartache of facing the sudden death of Dad's father, and the horrible murder of Dad's only brother. They faced difficult decisions concerning their own aging parents. They raised five sons to be honest, loyal, devout Christians, and respectable citizens. Just about everything Mom and Dad did, they did together.

The spiritual and emotional bond that developed between them was absolutely unbreakable. They were deeply in love with each other and remained completely faithful to each other for thirty-three years of marriage. They were totally committed to keeping the sacred vows which they had made on that summer day in 1956, "until death do us part."

The Sting of Death

I remember the phone call as though it were yesterday. It was December 13, 1989, Wednesday night. Susan and the kids and I were preparing to leave for church when the telephone rang. I answered it. It was my oldest brother Mark, and I could tell immediately that something was wrong. "Dad went to the doctor and they think he might have cancer. They won't know for sure until they do a biopsy," he said.

I didn't know what to say; I didn't know what to do; I didn't know what to think; I wasn't sure how to feel. Surely this can't be true. Dad is only ... *how old is Dad, anyway? I'm not sure, but he's not old enough to get cancer.* When someone gets cancer, they usually die. Dad can't die!

My head was spinning and my stomach was swimming as we went to church. "Maybe it won't be cancer after all," I kept telling myself, trying my best to sound convincing. "But what if it is?" We had just seen Mom and Dad a couple of weeks earlier. We had gone to Susan's parents' house in Round Rock for Thanksgiving. On the way back home, we stopped by Mom and Dad's house in Georgetown to say "Hi." Dad wasn't feeling well. He had started feeling sick the day after Thanksgiving, having stomach pains and feeling nauseated. He and Mom just figured he was coming down with an intestinal flu—there had been a lot of that sort of thing going around. After a week with no improvement, he went to see the doctor.

The doctor was unable to determine the cause of Dad's ailments, and arranged for some tests to be run in an attempt to pinpoint the problem. After running numerous tests and finding nothing, they finally did an ultrasound which revealed a number of suspicious-looking spots on his liver. A biopsy was ordered immediately.

The biopsy results were reported on Friday, December 15. The doctors' fears were confirmed. Dad had cancer. The initial prognosis was that he probably had six months to live.

Six months! I remember the shock, the horror, the disbelief, the fear, the complete sense of hopelessness and helplessness brought on by those two words: six months. Suddenly, life seemed so finite.

It was Christmas time. We were all supposed to be gathering at Mom and Dad's house in about a week for an O'Rear-style Christmas celebration. All five of us guys, our families, lots of presents, lots of love, lots of laughter, lots of good food…and Mom and Dad, the matriarch and patriarch of this uniquely wonderful clan.

But the trip came a week early, and the occasion was anything but festive. Dad was put in the hospital in Austin on Monday after the biopsy results had been reported on Friday. The doctors wanted to do more tests to determine a course of treatment. Now, instead of traveling to Georgetown for Christmas, we found ourselves traveling to Austin a week before Christmas to visit Dad in the hospital.

What would I say? What are you supposed to say to someone who has just been told they probably won't be here in six months? Dad was always the one who knew just what to say. And now he is the one lying in a hospital bed dying. Oh, God, help me know what to say. *Please, God, I'm so afraid. Please don't let my daddy die!*

As it turned out, Dad was still the one who knew just exactly what to say. "Boys…" He addressed his five sons.

We were the ones he and Mom had spent lots of years and lots of prayers raising.

We were the ones who had always caused people to look at Mom and say, "You poor woman!" In fact, people still say that to this day!

We were the ones who had spent many summers splashing around in the Frio River at River Bend Campground, during those wonderful family camping trips to the Texas hill country.

We were the ones who Dad and Mom had dragged—sometimes literally—to church every Sunday and every Wednesday of our lives.

And, we were the five young men who had learned to love the Lord, and his word, and his church—from the very depth of our being—because of this man who was now lying in a hospital bed dying, and because of the beautiful woman who stood by his side.

"Boys…" You could have heard a pin drop in that room as we hung on his words. "Mom and I have talked about this, and we want you to know that we are not afraid of what might happen. If it is God's will for me to die, then I am ready to die. Sure, I would love to stay around several more years and see my grandkids grow up. There are many things I would still like to do. I don't guess there will ever come a time when I could say, 'I've done everything I ever wanted to do and seen everything I ever wanted to see, so now I am ready to go.' But we want you boys to know that we are not asking, 'Why? Why us? Why this? Why now?' We are at peace."

In that moment, Dad left us a legacy that I will carry with me for the rest of my life. Dad was lying on his death bed, literally staring death in the face, and he was not the least bit afraid—or if he was, it certainly didn't show. He was truly at peace. Suddenly, all those things he had taught us through the years—about God, about his love for us, about heaven—it all became so very real in that one moment of time. Dad was about to go be with God, and he knew it!

Dad stayed in the hospital one week, and his condition quickly and progressively deteriorated. The doctors released him from the hospital on Sunday, Christmas Eve. He was groggy from the pain medication, as well as from the fact that his liver was not functioning properly due to the cancer. Monday and Tuesday his condition worsened further. He slept more and more and became less and less coherent. Tuesday night he had a very difficult night, and several of us stayed up all night with him.

Wednesday, December 27, 1989, was a day that Dad had spent his whole life preparing for. I remember it as being a peculiarly peaceful day. Everyone had left the house that morning. I don't remember who went where; I just remember that Mom and I were the only two in the house besides Dad. He was sleeping in his easy chair and we were just a few feet away, sitting at the kitchen table, talking about funeral arrangements. It was obvious that Dad would not be here much longer, and we wanted to be prepared. As we talked quietly, we could hear in the background the rhythmic sounds of Dad's breathing.

Then suddenly we both realized, in the same instant, that the breathing sounds had stopped. We jumped up and rushed over to the easy chair, but Dad was not there. His body was still in the chair, but Dad had gone Home.

Mom asked me gently and with remarkable composure if I would leave the room for a few minutes so she could be alone with him. I went to the back of the house, and Mom told Dad goodbye. His brief struggle had ended, and our struggle to go on living without him had begun.

Until Death Do Us Part

When Dad died in December of 1989, the words *until death do us part* became a haunting reality for Mom. They were no longer just hypothetical words spoken by young lovers as part of a fairy tale wedding. Death was the only thing that could have parted Mom and Dad, and after spending thirty-three years of their lives together, it became the only thing that did separate them.

Suddenly half of Mom's life was gone forever. Every night since then, Mom has gone to bed by herself, and every morning she awakens to an empty house. She sits in church every Sunday and Wednesday with no one's hand to hold. Those special songs that once triggered floods of wonderful memories of romantic times spent together, now somehow seem to have a haunting emptiness about them.

For the last several years of Dad's life, he and Mom worked for the same company and often drove to work together. After Dad died, Mom had to drive to work all alone every day. Dad's exuberant and contagious cheerfulness no longer brightened the company halls. The job, which had once been simply another piece of the beautiful life they were building together, suddenly became just one more reminder of the palpable emptiness that accompanied Dad's absence. In time, that emptiness became unbearable, and Mom found a new job.

My point is this. For thirty-three years, Mom and Dad shared every joy and every heartache of life together. In December of 1989 that changed forever. Every day since then, Mom has lived with the constant nagging heartache of realizing that she will never be able to share those things with Dad again for the entire rest of her life. Dad is gone from this place for good. He is not coming back. Life can never be the same for Mom. She cannot just "get over it."

The E-mail

About a year after Ashley's death, my precious mother sent me an e-mail saying that she would like to find some time to sit down and talk with Susan about grieving, just the two of them. Mom had learned from some other family members that Susan still seemed to be having a very difficult time with Ashley's death. She was also concerned that Susan and I might not be taking care of ourselves in our grief like we needed to be. With Mom's permission, I want to share with you some excerpts from my response to her e-mail.

> Dear Mom,
>
> Yes, Susan is still having a hard time with Ashley's death. I am still having a hard time with Ashley's death. Justin is still having a hard time with Ashley's death. We will *always* have a hard time with Ashley's death. Our precious, precious child is gone from our arms forever. We can never kiss her beautiful little bald head again. We can never again take her shopping and push her around in her wheelchair. We can never again see that incredibly infectious smile that could melt (and often did melt) even the hardest of hearts. We can never again lie in bed with her and have tickle fights. Susan will never, ever, ever, ever be able to do "Mother-Daughter" things…ever. Her only daughter is dead and gone at age fourteen, and nothing will ever bring her back. That hole is simply not "fillable."

For four long years, almost every day of our lives centered in some way around taking care of Ashley. We can't take care of her anymore. We will not get to watch her graduate from high school, or from Texas A&M. I will never get to walk her down the aisle at her wedding. Half of our grandchildren will never be born. And on and on and on and on and on the list could go ... and does go ... and will go ... for the entire rest of our lives, until the very day we die.

Ashley is gone forever from this earth. My daddy heart breaks all over again every single day because she is gone and I can't hold her. Susan's mommy heart breaks all over again every single day because Ashley is gone and she can't hold her. Broken hearts, by their very nature, are extremely painful and produce lots of tears.

As far as us not taking care of ourselves in our grief like we need to, I actually think we are doing a pretty good job of taking care of ourselves. (And please don't misinterpret that as my "taking issue" with your concern, or anything like that. Susan and I both appreciate your concern, and everyone's concern, more than we could ever adequately express. We are tremendously blessed, and Ashley was tremendously blessed, to be part of this wonderful, loving family. The love and concern that everyone has shown in so many ways has been such an incredible blessing to us. We wouldn't trade our places in this family for all the money in the world. I love you more than you could possibly imagine, Mom; and everything you have done for us, and everything you are, cause me to thank God every day for giving me the best mommy in the world!)

Taking care of ourselves certainly doesn't mean that we have conquered our tears. On the contrary, tears are the natural response to pain, and pain is an everyday reality for us. Sometimes our tears are uncontrollable, because the pain is unbearable. But I am convinced that our hearts are supposed to be broken. There is no way around that reality. No amount of grief support, or grief counseling, or grief processing, or taking care of ourselves, or anything else can ever make the pain in our hearts go away. It can't be done. It is impossible. And I don't want the pain in my heart to go away! The only way to make that happen would be for Ashley to walk back into our lives and our arms ... and that's not going to happen. And to be perfectly honest, I don't really even want that to happen, because that would require taking her away from heaven, and I don't think I could bring myself to do that even if I were to find a way.

Susan and I both cry an awful lot. Often the tears come unexpectedly, triggered by some little insignificant something, or by nothing at all. Sometimes we are together when those moments hit. Often we are by ourselves, moving in the many different directions that our busy lives carry us throughout the course of a day. Sometimes the sudden recurrence of familiar heartache is overwhelming and brings everything to a screeching halt, temporarily. And then we regain composure and control for the time being, and carry on. That's just the way life works now. And it's OK. Honestly, it is. Underneath it all, we are both pretty emotionally healthy and stable (mostly from good raising, I imagine!). That underlying emotional stability allows us to accept those frequent moments of seemingly unbearable pain, to give in to the uncontrollable flow of tears, and then to move on to the next task of the day.

A heart broken by grief simply cannot be "fixed." The emptiness of grief does not go away. The pain and heartache do not magically disappear after a certain amount of grieving time or after successfully completing each step of some generically-prescribed "grieving process." And so, what one must learn to do is not to search for "healing" for his grief-stricken heart, because healing implies a completed process in which the offending symptom (in this case the pain of grief) is successfully eradicated from the victim. Rather, I believe the healthier and more realistic approach is to figure out how to go on living, and experiencing all that life has to offer, and rediscovering happiness … *with* a broken heart. I think we've got to learn to accept the pain and allow it to have its place in our lives in healthy and even productive ways, rather than trying to figure out how to process the pain out of our lives.

I guess I've said all that to simply say this … we are doing OK. We hurt, we cry, we move on. Sometimes this may appear to be unhealthy, or it may appear that we are not OK, or that we are not handling our grief appropriately, or that we have not adequately recovered from our grief in a reasonable amount of time, or something else like that. Actually, most of the time it's probably just frustrating because people have the tendency—when they see someone in pain—to want to "fix something" and make the pain go away. But we know that the pain can't be fixed, and that it ain't going away. So we just accept it, deal with it, and go on living. A pretty healthy approach, I think. And it's really the only way I know to approach it. So to those who are concerned about us and want to fix our pain, we really appreciate it. But we also want everyone to know that it simply isn't possible to fix the pain and make it go away…and that's OK, and *we* are OK.

And much of that we learned from Ashley.

Horace Bratcher

They say that time heals all wounds, but I have come to believe that some wounds are not supposed to heal. When you lose someone whom you dearly love, time does allow you to develop the ability to cope with the emptiness. But no amount of time can possibly make the emptiness go away. In fact, I believe that the deep emptiness that has been left in our lives by Dad's death and by Ashley's death is a wonderful tribute to the incredible people they were. Their absence hurts so much because their presence brought so much joy.

Horace Bratcher is a dear friend and Christian brother. He is also a self-educated philosopher. He makes frequent trips to the local library to sit and read.

In his readings, he is constantly looking for memorable quotes and sayings that help to explain something about life in a way that is easily understandable. Several days a week, Horace stops by my office to share his latest philosophical discoveries and ponderings. I have learned many valuable lessons through the years from our weekly chats.

One day as Horace and I were talking, the subject of grief came up. I explained to him some of my philosophy concerning grief, and he shared some of his. We discussed this idea that *time heals all wounds*. I explained my belief that some wounds are not supposed to heal, no matter how much time passes. In response, Horace shared with me something that he had read concerning this very subject. It is a tremendous analogy that makes a whole lot of sense. He said, "Grief is like a deep wound. In time the pain may subside and the wound may heal over, but there will always be a scar."

My discussions with many people who are at various stages in their own personal journeys of grief have led me to believe that Horace—and whomever he quoted—is exactly right. Immediately following a loss, the sheer intensity of grief may seem unbearable. The weight on the griever's heart may be so heavy that it seems life may never again be joyful; there may never again be laughter; there is no light at the end of the tunnel, and perhaps there doesn't even seem to be any reason to go on living. This corresponds to the deep, open, festering wound in Horace's analogy, and the pain that is brought by such a wound.

The further one moves from the moment of loss, however, the less intense the grief becomes. This may not even be noticeable for a while, but with time comes the ability to once again carry out the daily functions of life. At some point, the griever is able to focus again on paying the bills, shopping for groceries, doing laundry, concentrating on the necessary tasks at work without being constantly distracted by the emptiness and pain in his own mind and heart. With time, daily routines return to normal. Life begins to settle back down. Things start to make sense again. This corresponds to the healing of the wound in Horace's analogy.

However, there will probably always be moments, no matter how far you have traveled down grief's difficult road, when the pain returns. It may be sparked by a song on the radio, a show or even a commercial advertisement on television, the comment of a friend, attendance at someone else's funeral, a comment made in church by the preacher, or even just a happy memory of your loved one.

In my own experience, I have noticed that those momentary relapses of pain can be very intense, even emotionally debilitating. Though each passing day moves me further and further away from the actual moment of Ashley's death, sometimes a wave of heartache can hit me like a ton of bricks, seemingly out of nowhere. At times the pain can seem as intense as the day Ashley died. I am momentarily rendered completely useless. But after a short time I am able to regain my composure and continue whatever I was doing.

From Horace's analogy, this is the scar. The wound may be healing over. It may not be as gaping and fresh as when it was inflicted. It may, at some point, even heal over completely; but even if that happens, there will always be a scar. There will always be a reminder that once there was a gaping, festering wound. There will always be an emptiness in my heart that from time to time will rise up and remind me that it is there. Then, satisfied that I remember, it will subside and patiently wait for the next moment to manifest itself—maybe tomorrow, maybe next week, maybe next year. But it will always find another opportunity to show itself.

It is interesting to note that the triggers for these relapses of emotional pain may not be consistent. There have been moments when a particular song has reduced me to a useless blob of tears. The next time I hear that same song, it may simply produce a peaceful sense of nostalgia, or even trigger a flood of happy memories. The same song may, at the same time, create one response in me and a totally different response in Susan. Such is the unpredictable nature of grief.

As my life takes me further away from the day Ashley left this world for her eternal home, I have become better able to carry on the demanding duties of work and everyday life in spite of the emptiness created by her loss. Those moments of relapse seem to be getting further apart, even though any particular relapse has the potential to be powerfully intense. The pain has not gone away. It is simply moving from a place of prominence in the foreground of my life, where it started when Ashley died, to a less conspicuous place somewhere in the background. There will always be a scar. There will always be an emptiness. There will always be something missing. But I am learning better each day how to go on living, and loving, and laughing, and remembering ... *with* a broken heart.

A Simple Hug

Next time you are tempted to advise someone who is grieving to "get over it and get on with your life," may I suggest that you simply offer a hug instead? You see, "getting over it" is not even an option.

Other People's Expectations

I f you are reading this book, not because of your own broken heart, but because someone you love is grieving, or perhaps because you just want to learn more about the grieving process, let me ask you a few questions. If you are the brokenhearted one, please bear with me for just a moment. This is important.

Based upon what you have heard or read in the past, or upon what you currently understand about grief and the grieving process, how would you answer the following questions?

1. What are the stages that most people experience as they work through the grieving process? Denial? Despair? Depression? Anger? Lack of motivation? Lethargy?

2. How long should the grieving process typically last? One month? Three months? Six months? Surely by the time a year has passed, the grieving process will have been completed.

3. What are the signs that someone is not handling their grief properly? At what point should you lovingly suggest that they seek counseling to help them get through their grief?

4. What are the right things to say to a person who is grieving? Should you avoid talking about their

deceased loved one, because you do not want to cause any further pain?

I'm sure you have wondered about some or all of these things at one point or another when someone you care about is grieving.

Please pay careful attention to what I say next. This may fly in the face of everything you have ever heard or believed concerning the grieving process. Nevertheless, the following paragraph represents a substantial part of my core belief concerning grief:

> There is no such thing as a pre-defined "grieving process." There is no universal, one-size-fits-all formula for grieving or grief management. No two people grieve in exactly the same way. A person who is not grieving is in no position to place his or her pre-conceived expectations upon the person who is grieving.

Therefore, in my humble opinion, the first two questions posed above can be thrown out, because the questions themselves are based on false assumptions and therefore actually have the potential to cause more harm than good.

The Stages of Grief

My wife Susan became rather frustrated shortly after Ashley's death because of a question that a well-meaning friend asked her. "Have you gone through the stage yet where you are angry at God?" Neither

Susan nor I blame God for Ashley's death. We never became angry at God for not allowing her to live past the age of fourteen. We did not "lose our religion," nor did our faith suffer because of Ashley's death. Rather, our faith has grown stronger, because we have chosen to deal with our grief within the context of that faith. God is not the enemy. He is the ultimate source of comfort, and the only one who can provide any type of true healing for our broken hearts. We skipped the anger stage. Or perhaps we simply missed the memo that said there was even supposed to *be* an anger stage.

Our reaction to the "angry with God" question was really little more than minor annoyance. We realized that the person asking the question had wonderful, caring intentions, but was simply misinformed, as are so many people. The fact that such a question was asked, however, does point to a frustrating reality when it comes to grief.

I believe there are many people who have the expectation that everyone's grief is a similar experience; that there is a "grieving process," or a universal formula which clearly defines the road that every grieving person travels. We have all heard something about the "stages of grief," and have probably been led to believe that everyone who grieves passes through each of those stages in sequential order. It was only natural, then, for the "anger stage" question to be asked, because anger with God is one of those pre-defined stages in the grieving process…right? Wrong!

There is no such thing as a pre-defined "grieving process." There is no universal, one-size-fits-all formula for grieving or grief management. No two people grieve in exactly the same way.

Grief is a very personal experience. Your grief belongs to you and to no one else. My grief belongs to me, and to no one else. There is no guarantee that even my wife and I will share the exact same grief experience, even though we are both grieving for the same reason, the death of our daughter Ashley.

Susan and I are not the same person. We think differently, we react differently to various situations, and our emotional make-up is vastly different. My relationship with Ashley, as her daddy, was not exactly the same as Susan and Ashley's mother-daughter relationship. The things that I miss about Ashley are not necessarily the exact same things that Susan misses about Ashley. There have been times when some little incident reminds us of Ashley, and Susan responds with a nostalgic grin, while my response is with tears, or vice versa.

No one told Susan's and my hearts that there was some pre-programmed course of action that our hearts were supposed to follow in dealing with the grief of losing our precious daughter. We simply take life, and grief, one day at a time, and sometimes one moment at a time. If my heart tells me that I need to cry, then I cry. If my heart tells me that I need to smile or laugh, then I smile or laugh. On days when my heart feels an inescapably heavy emptiness because I miss Ashley so much that I am rendered completely useless, I simply accept the fact that such inescapably heavy emptiness is what is right for my heart at that moment in time, whether it fits anyone else's prefabricated grief formula for me or not.

There may be similarities in your grief experience and another person's grief experience. That is fine. Or, you may find that your grief experience follows a completely different emotional path than every other person's grief experience. That is also fine. Your grief experience belongs to you and to you alone. No one has the right to place their expectations upon you concerning the stages of grief you should experience, the time frame in which you should be able to successfully graduate from the grieving process and "get on with your life," or any other aspect of dealing with your grief. As far as I am concerned, you have an inalienable right to grieve in your own way, and at your own pace.

Grief's Timetable

When my dad died of cancer at age fifty-eight, leaving my mom a widow after thirty-three years of marriage, I learned a lot about grief not only from my own personal experience with the grief of losing my dad; I also learned a lot about grief by observing my mom's experience. On one occasion, a well-meaning little old lady from church made a statement to my mom that went something like this: "Bettie, it's been six months since Larry died. Don't you think it's time you got over it and got on with your life?"

Similar to people's expectations about the stages of grief, some people also have pre-conceived notions about how long the grieving process should last. Naturally, the heartache will be most agonizing right at first. But, as time goes on, shouldn't the grieving person be able to gradually put their grief behind them and get on with their life? The answer to that question is both simple and complex.

The simple answer is an emphatic *No!* The heartache of losing a loved one does not simply vanish with time. You cannot just put your grief behind you and go on with life as though it never happened.

If you were involved in an automobile accident that resulted in your right arm being severed, do you think that life could possibly ever be "normal" again? Of course not! If you were right-handed prior to the accident, you would have to train yourself to write with your left hand, to eat with your left hand, to do everything with your left hand. You would have to teach yourself to tie your shoes using only one hand, to type using only one hand, to ride a bicycle or drive a car using only one hand, to dress yourself using only one hand, and to do everything else that was once a two-handed task using only one hand.

It is true that, with time, you would develop increased ability and proficiency in performing all those tasks. But would life ever be the same as it was when you had two arms and two hands? Absolutely not. Your right arm is gone for good. It is never going to grow back. For the entire rest of your life, you will be a one-armed person living in a world designed for people with two arms.

While writing this book, one night I saw a television documentary about a lady named Mary who had been raped as a teenager, and then had both of her arms cut off by her attacker. Shortly after the attack, she was fitted with prosthetic arms. For the rest of her life, Mary was forced not only to deal with the trauma of having been so brutally raped and attacked, she also had to relearn how to do everything that required the use of arms and hands.

Life was never the same for Mary, and there was nothing she could do about it. She could not go back and change the past. She could not just ignore the fact that she was raped or that she had lost both arms. She could not just "get over it and get on with her life." Part of her was now missing, and now she had to relearn how to live life without arms and hands. When you have to start over and relearn how to live life, it can be a very time-consuming and frustrating process.

The same is true with grief. For my mom, life would never be the same after my dad's death, and there was nothing she could do about it. She could not go back and change the past. She could not just ignore the fact that Dad was gone. Part of her was missing, and now she had to relearn how to live life without Dad. When you have to start over and relearn how to live life, it can be a very time-consuming and frustrating process.

For Susan and Justin and me, life will never be the same after Ashley's death, and there is nothing we can do about it. We cannot go back and change the past. We cannot just ignore the fact that Ashley is no longer here with us. Part of us is missing, and now we have to relearn how to live life without Ashley. When you have to start over and relearn how to live life, it can be a very time-consuming and frustrating process.

As time passes, my ability to cope with Ashley's death increases, and the days on which I am rendered utterly useless by the unbearable emptiness of my heavy heart come further and further apart. But down deep in my soul I know that, even though time brings a measure of healing, complete healing is something I will never achieve. My heart will never be completely unbroken— not three months from now, not six months from now, not a year from now, and not even twenty years from now. Even when I am sixty-five or seventy years old and have a grandchild who is fourteen, deep inside my heart there will still be a thirty-nine-year-old daddy who just lost the only princess he ever had. That will never go away.

Timothy Hill's Daddy

The truth of that reality was driven home one Sunday night when a couple from New York came to visit our church congregation in Texas. This couple, the Hills, had established a boys' ranch in New York in memory of their son Timothy. Timothy was killed at age thirteen when he was hit by a truck while riding his bicycle to school.[1] Our congregation had provided financial support to the ranch for years, and the Hills had come to give us a report on the ranch's work.

I listened intently as Mr. Hill began to explain the history of the ranch. As a little boy, Timothy had told his parents about a dream of his to one day build a ranch for kids who needed a place to live. When Timothy died, the family decided to adopt his dream as their own, and to make that dream come true. They built Timothy's ranch for underprivileged boys, and named it in Timothy's honor.

When Mr. Hill got to the point in the story where he was telling about Timothy's accident and his death, there was a noticeable quiver in his voice. This was some thirty years after Timothy's death. All of the other Hill children were now grown and on their own with their own families. Mr. and Mrs. Hill were grandparents. And yet, when Mr. Hill recounted the story of Timothy's death, in his mind little Timmy was still just thirteen years old, and in his daddy heart there was a broken emptiness that still had not vanished. Even thirty years was not enough time to fill the hole in his heart. Grieving truly is a never-ending process. There is no timetable for overcoming grief because grief is simply not designed to be overcome.

Handling Grief Appropriately

One of the most frustrating things about losing a loved one is the expectations of other people concerning the appropriate ways in which to deal with your grief.

If you cry too much or for too long, people may be inclined to think that you are slipping into an unhealthy depression and that you may need counseling or drugs to help you get over it and get on with your life.

If you laugh too much or too soon, people may be inclined to think that you are suppressing your grief in unhealthy ways and that you may need counseling or drugs to help you be able express your grief in appropriate ways, so that it does not all stay bottled up inside you.

I am not saying that there is no place in this world for grief counselors, or even for antidepressants and other drugs, which may help some people who are truly having difficulty functioning because of their grief. Even though the heartache of grief cannot be eradicated, the grieving person certainly does need to find the strength to continue living and functioning and carrying on with the tasks which are necessary for daily life. If professional counseling or prescription drugs can help the grieving person in that regard, that is wonderful. Getting over it is not an option, but getting on with your life certainly is.

The whole premise of this book is the idea that one can continue to *live—with* a broken heart. The brokenness of one's heart cannot be taken away, but life does go on. One must continue to work so that the bills can continue to be paid. In our case, we lost our daughter, but we still have a son who needs our love and attention and guidance on a daily basis. Interaction with other people continues to be a necessity for healthy living, even when one is overcome with grief.

When the grieving person fails to once again practice these normal, essential, healthy components of daily living, then concern is valid. In such a situation, it may even be necessary for a concerned family member or friend to intervene and attempt to get the grieving person some help so that they can get back to carrying on with their life. My only advice is to not be too quick in jumping to the conclusion that intervention is needed.

Each person is different, and each person will handle their grief differently. Do not try to impose what you consider to be "universally appropriate measures" on any particular person who is grieving. Let me give you a couple of examples to clarify what I am saying.

The Stretcher and the Pills

Ashley died on Saturday afternoon. She had been sleeping in Susan's and my bed Friday night as her condition gradually deteriorated. She died in our bed, with both of us by her side. After the authorities were notified, it took some time for the justice of the peace and the coroner to arrive, pronounce Ashley dead, and remove her body from our house. That whole series of events is somewhat of a fog in my memory. However, I remember very vividly the moment at which Ashley's body was carried through our kitchen on a stretcher in a body bag to be placed in the coroner's vehicle. Our emotions were running high, and it was certainly a moment in time when we were at a pinnacle of our grief.

Notice I said "a pinnacle," not "the pinnacle." I believe grief comes in waves, or in mountains and valleys. There can be many pinnacle moments, each one just as high or as deep as the previous one or the one to come.

As the stretcher was approaching the kitchen where Susan and I were both standing, some well-meaning family members and friends attempted to screen us from seeing the stretcher with Ashley's body being removed from the house. I'm sure someone had either read or heard that seeing such a sight could be a traumatic experience, and should be avoided if at all possible. Being the stubborn person that I am, I refused to comply. I purposely turned and watched as the officials carried Ashley's body through the house. There was something inside of me that told me I needed to witness her final exit from our family's home. Maybe some people would not be able to handle such a scene, but I am not "some people." I am me, and this was my precious daughter whose lifeless body was being removed from my home forever, never to return. I *needed* to see that. Why? I don't know. But I needed to. Maybe some experts have fooled people into believing some "universal principle" that no grieving parent should ever witness such a sight, but if that is the case then the experts are wrong! I refused to be sucked into someone else's idea of what was appropriate or not appropriate for me in my time of grief.

That same afternoon, another well-meaning attempt was made to help us cope as our world was falling apart around us. It was assumed that Susan would need some assistance, in the form of drugs, to be able to sleep through the night. One of our doctor friends was called and asked to provide a prescription for some sleeping pills. Susan repeatedly refused to take the pills at first, but finally gave in to the persistent insistence that she take them, just so that everyone would quit bugging her. Shortly after taking one pill, she fell asleep in the middle of a telephone conversation. Moments later, she awoke suddenly and began lurching toward the bathroom because she felt extremely nauseated. She was hardly even able to walk, due to the sedating effect of the medicine. After she threw up in the toilet, I carried her back to the bed, helped her get into her pajamas, and tucked her in for the night.

It was assumed that, because of Susan's grief, she would not be able to sleep. Even though she insisted that she was fine, others insisted that she was not. The generic expectation that someone in the throes of grief needs help sleeping was foisted upon Susan, even against her insistence that such an expectation was not realistic and did not apply to her. I foolishly almost caused a split in our family that night because of my angry reaction to the way Susan had been forced to take that medicine against her will. Thankfully, we were able to resolve the situation, and our extended family remains intact.

These examples show the potential harm that can be done when generalized expectations concerning grief are applied to every grieving person universally, without consideration given to that person's own individual strength and emotional constitution. During the four years between Ashley's original cancer diagnosis and her death, both Susan and I had grown exponentially in our emotional strength and our ability to handle unbelievably difficult situations. This was a direct result of the daily battle against Ashley's cancer.

We had walked through the valley of the shadow of death with Ashley on several occasions, the last one just about a week prior to her death.

Joe's Crab Shack

Ashley had been having trouble swallowing due to the effects of the growing tumors in her brain. On one particular evening, we had gone with some dear friends, the Neal White family, to Joe's Crab Shack, one of Ashley's favorite places to eat. Near the end of the meal Ashley needed to go to the bathroom, so Susan accompanied her, pushing her in her wheelchair.

Ashley had been chewing on a piece of shrimp for quite some time. While in the bathroom, she tried to swallow it and it became lodged in her throat. She started choking. Susan immediately got Ashley up out of the wheelchair and tried to do the Heimlich maneuver. It didn't work, and Ashley continued choking.

Susan took Ashley out of the bathroom and began asking for help. Everyone just looked at them. Ashley was unable to get any air, and was beginning to turn blue. Susan could see in her eyes a frantic pleading. "Please help me, Mom!" Nothing Susan tried worked, and no one was offering any help. Ashley was dying right in front of Susan's eyes, and there was nothing she could do to help her.

Meanwhile, I was sitting at the table with Neal and his family, not aware that anything was wrong until Neal's youngest son came back to the table and said that Ashley was choking. When I got to where Ashley was, she was lying on the floor near the restroom entrance, unconscious and turning purple. Her eyes were open and glazed over. Susan was sitting a few feet away curled up in a fetal position, screaming hysterically.

A young man named Joe finally came rushing over from the bar area to help us. He identified himself as a paramedic who was working a second job at Joe's Crab Shack, asked me about Ashley's medical condition, and then proceeded to perform the Heimlich maneuver with Ashley still lying unconscious on the floor. With the second or third thrust, he successfully dislodged the piece of shrimp that was blocking her airway. Ashley immediately regained consciousness.

A few moments later an ambulance arrived—someone had called 9-1-1—and took Ashley to Children's Medical Center to be checked out. She was released after a few hours in the emergency room. We went home, weary and worn, but thankful to be taking Ashley home with us.

Battle-Hardened

After Ashley's initial brain surgery, we had sat with her in ICU, watching helplessly as she lay there with tubes hanging out of her head and countless wires and gadgets attached to her body. Throughout her cancer battle, we had scrambled on many occasions in the middle of the night to get her to the hospital quickly because her body temperature had risen to dangerous levels. We had watched her dwindle to almost nothing when she went through a stage where she quit eating, as the doctors struggled to find the right way to provide her with nourishment.

On one occasion, we even made a post-midnight run to the hospital to change out a feeding tube that had been surgically implanted through the wall of her stomach. The tube had begun leaking profusely, and we could not get it to stop. We were scheduled to fly out to Florida for Ashley's Make-A-Wish trip to Disney World just a few hours later that morning. The trip seemed in jeopardy, and the emotional toll that would have been taken on Ashley if we missed that trip was completely unacceptable. We got her to the hospital, got the tube changed, made it back to the hotel for a couple of hours of sleep, and caught our plane on schedule.

I could fill page after page with similar stories. With each incident, our capacity to handle adversity had been stretched. We had become battle-hardened. We were emotionally tough. We had dealt with many, many difficult situations and had survived and even been made stronger as a result.

Helping Your Friend Grieve

Our situation was unique. We were not like everyone else. In fact, no one is like everyone else! Every single grieving person has their own particular strengths and weaknesses. They each have their own unique personalities and experiences in dealing with life's tough situations. No two people are alike, and so it only makes sense that there cannot possibly be a set of universally-standard practices and procedures for dealing with grief. If someone you love is brokenhearted because of grief, give them the benefit of the doubt. Do not assume that all the rules you have heard or read about concerning grief, and concerning what you need to do to help someone who is grieving, apply to your friend or loved one.

Allow your grieving friend or loved one to determine what they are able to handle, and what they are not able to handle, in dealing with their own grief. Don't tell them what they need to do or don't need to do based on what you have read or heard concerning grief.

If you see that problems are arising because your friend or loved one is unable to begin functioning normally again and carrying out the necessary tasks of daily living, carefully and prayerfully look for ways to gently help them back onto the path of productive living. The first step may be to simply provide assistance with some of those nagging daily tasks. As time goes on, however, they need to gradually step back into the pilot's seat of their own daily routines. When that transition fails to take place, professional help may be useful or even necessary.

Be there to help but be careful not to be too pushy in imposing your expectations upon them. This can be a very difficult and tricky tightrope to walk. I understand that. It can be extremely frustrating trying to find the right balance, trying to determine exactly when your friend has reached a point where intervention is needed. But that is simply the nature of grief. No one said it was going to be easy.

Love, I believe, is the great balancer. Love and restraint, working together, will help you find the right ways to help your friend in their grief. Be there to help. Be supportive. Look for ways you can help with daily tasks. Silently watch for signs that the grief may be taking an unhealthy and dangerous toll on the griever's daily responsibilities. If intervention is needed, proceed with gentleness and great caution in facilitating that intervention.

May God bless you as you try to help your friend or loved one deal with their loss, without creating an additional burden on them in the form of unrealistic expectations.

Grieve in Your Own Way

There is no such thing as a pre-defined "grieving process." There is no universal, one-size-fits-all formula for grieving or grief management. No two people grieve in exactly the same way. A person who is not grieving is in no position to place his or her pre-conceived expectations upon the person who is grieving.

N o two people grieve in exactly the same way. Your grief is yours and yours alone. You are the only person on earth who knows exactly what is right for you on your grief journey.

What Do We Do With Her Stuff?

Often the question arises when a loved one dies, and perhaps especially when a child dies, "What are we supposed to do with all her stuff?" My answer would be that there is *nothing* that you are *supposed* to do with your deceased loved one's stuff. There is no universal principle that requires the same action on the part of every person who finds himself or herself faced with such a difficult dilemma.

I have known of families who have left their deceased child's bedroom completely untouched, exactly as she left it, as though she would pop in the front door at any moment, announce "I'm home from school," and make her way to her room to play with her dolls and do her homework.

I have known of other families who could not bear to hold on to their deceased loved one's belongings, because seeing their child's toys or clothes or collectibles only served to spark powerful memories which resulted in deep pain. So they chose to sell or give away or throw away everything that reminded them of their child. Which of these is the right response to a loved one's death? I do not believe there is one response that is right for everyone. I believe everyone should be allowed to grieve in their own way.

Ashley had lots of stuff! She absolutely loved Beanie Babies and was always on the lookout for the newest one or for one that she did not already have. Every time she was admitted to Children's Medical Center, her first order of business after getting settled into her room was to make a trip to the gift shop where her buddies Faye and Rose—the ladies who ran the gift shop—were always happy to see her. Ashley was probably their best customer, but these precious ladies and Ashley had developed a deep friendship that was a blessing to all three of them, and that went far beyond any mere retailer-customer relationship.

It just so happened that the hospital gift shop sold Beanie Babies, which is why it also just so happened that the gift shop was one of Ashley's favorite places on earth. She could spend hours looking at the new Beanie Babies, holding them, and carefully deciding which one to buy on this particular shopping excursion.

It was a much-needed diversion from the harsh reality of hospital life.

When Ashley was not stuck in the hospital in Dallas, one of her most-uttered phrases was, "I want to go to the Briarpatch." The Briarpatch is a small, local boutique gift shop, so packed full of every imaginable collectible and unique gift and silly whatnot that there is barely room to move through the shop.

Ashley adored Kirsti, the shop's owner, who always had something new to show her. And yes, Kirsti sold Beanie Babies. A trip to the Briarpatch was like a field trip to heaven for Ashley, and she pitted the Briarpatch and the hospital gift shop in an unofficial friendly competition to see who could provide her with the best selection of Beanie Babies to add to her collection.

In addition to the Beanie Babies (and Pillow Pals and Mini Beanie Babies), Ashley had amassed quite a collection of other stuffed animals and plush toys. Some were gifts that had been sent to her from other states—and even other countries—from people who were following Ashley's story on the Internet.

She had a handcrafted dollhouse that had been made especially for her by members of an online miniatures club. Then she began receiving miniature furniture, miniature people, miniature wall hangings, miniature toys and games, and lots of other items to completely furnish her dollhouse. Each day's trip to the mailbox was like Christmas! These goodies came from people, once again, all over the world.

Ashley loved to read, and especially enjoyed the *Goosebumps* series of books by R. L. Stine. She developed quite a collection of books that filled an entire bookshelf in her bedroom. She had lots of t-shirts, lots of hats, lots of souvenirs ... in short, she had lots and lots of stuff!

When Ashley died, we really did not even consider the question of "What do we do with all her stuff?" For a while, her room remained just like she had left it. It was not that we made a conscious decision to leave everything like it was. I really don't believe the thought even crossed our minds, for quite some time, that we needed to make a decision. Ashley's stuff was there, so by default it just stayed there.

After some time had passed, we let Justin move into Ashley's room because it was bigger than his room. We moved all of Ashley's stuff into Justin's old room, boxing up some of it because it did not all fit.

From time to time, Susan or I would decide to give some particular item of Ashley's to someone for whom it would have special meaning. We always checked with each other to make sure we were both okay with any particular gifting. One of the worst things a husband and wife could do as they travel the road of grief together would be to create an emotional chasm between themselves because one spouse gave away something that the other one really wanted to keep due to a strong sentimental attachment.

On numerous occasions, Susan would sit and go through one or more boxes of Ashley's stuff and say something like, "We really need to get rid of some of this stuff. There is no sense in having all this stuff just sitting around in boxes. But I can't get rid of this (holding up a particular t-shirt), and I can't get rid of this (holding up one of Ashley's favorite hats), and I can't get rid of this (holding up a stuffed animal)." I felt no particular compulsion to get rid of anything, so I always tried to reassure her that it was okay for us to keep whatever of Ashley's things, and as much of it, as we wanted to.

A very dear friend of ours once told us that it was unhealthy for us to keep all of Ashley's things. She, too, had lost a child, and apparently the right course of action for her was to get rid of her son's belongings. That's fine, but that does not make such a choice right for everyone else. And it certainly did not make it the right choice for us.

Even ten years after Ashley's death, we still have a lot of Ashley's prized possessions in our house. They mean something to us, because they meant something to her. There is certainly nothing wrong or unhealthy with our decision to hang onto Ashley's things. It is what is right for us in our grief journey. And it certainly has not kept us from living emotionally healthy, stable, and productive lives.

No two people grieve in exactly the same way. Your grief is yours and yours alone. You are the only person on earth who knows exactly what is right for you on your grief journey.

Seeking Support

I mentioned earlier the importance of being careful not to make too quick a decision that a grieving friend needs professional help in dealing with their grief. However, if you are the one grieving and you decide that it would be helpful for you to seek the services of a professional grief counselor, follow your instinct. Do not feel like there is something wrong with you just because you need some help sorting out all of the emotional turmoil that you are experiencing in your time of grief. That is why grief counselors exist, to simply help you sort it all out.

For some people, finding encouragement, understanding, and support among other grievers can be very valuable as they navigate the tricky waters of loss and grief. There are numerous support groups that exist— some strictly local and some part of a larger nationwide network—that are designed to provide just such encouragement, understanding, and support. Some of these are very specific in the type of loss they support. The Compassionate Friends is for those who have lost a child. Alliance of Hope is for those who have lost someone to suicide. Others are more generically designed to help anyone who is grieving.

If seeking the guidance of a grief counselor or participating in a grief support group seems right for you, there are various ways you can find just such a counselor or group. If you know someone else who is grieving, ask them if they are aware of any grief support groups or grief counselors nearby. If they have participated in such a group themselves, or have sought the services of a professional grief counselor, perhaps they can provide more specific information about their experiences and even recommend a particular group or counselor.

If you are a member of a church or other religious organization, check with your minister or other spiritual leader for a recommendation. Churches and other religious groups often keep information on file regarding grief support services that their members might find helpful.

Start asking around in your local medical community. Hospitals often employ Social Workers, and they can be a great source of information concerning available grief support options. If there is a hospice agency in your town or city, they might be a good source of information as well.

Another potential resource is the Internet. Simply Google the phrase "grief support" or "grief counseling," and then spend some time perusing the results.

One thing that you need to remember, if you decide to participate in a grief support group or seek professional counseling, is that you are still the ultimate authority on exactly what is right for you on your grief journey. Go into the session with an open mind, realizing that you may be exposed to some new ideas or philosophies or coping mechanisms that could be beneficial; but do not feel obligated to accept everything that is suggested—especially in a group setting—as being right for you.

One good thing about support groups is that, in addition to receiving support from others who are also grieving, you have the opportunity to provide encouragement, understanding and support to others as well.

Larry Barber, in his book *Love Never Dies: Embracing Grief with Hope and Promise*, gives a very helpful list of questions to ask when searching for a grief support group.[1] Larry himself is a Licensed Professional Counselor certified in Thanatology (the specialized study of death, dying and bereavement). He is also a fellow griever, having lost his wife and daughter in a horrible auto accident in 1993.[2] His book contains many helpful insights for those who decide to seek professional grief counseling or join a grief support group, as well as many practical suggestions for dealing with grief.

Susan and I chose not to seek out a grief counselor or grief support group when we lost Ashley. We did not feel like that was a necessary element to our own personal grief journey. We had a tremendous support system already in place with our family, friends, and church family, and we were not completely comfortable with the idea of walking into a group of strangers and baring our souls and exposing our rawest emotions.

Grief support groups and grief counselors can be a tremendous help for many people, but they are not right for everyone. You are the only person on earth who knows exactly what is right for you on your grief journey.

Creative Outlets for Your Grief

Finding a creative outlet for your grief can be very cathartic. As in everything we have discussed here, your grief is yours alone, and only you can determine what is right for you in your grief journey. It may be that none of the following suggestions are a good fit for you, and that is perfectly okay. My hope, however, is that something mentioned here will spark an idea that will lead you to finding one or more creative ways to express your grief. Not only can such an exercise be therapeutic for you, your creative expression of grief might just provide a glimmer of hope for a fellow grief-traveler, or a sense of peace, or at least a realization that "I'm not alone." You may discover a way to help others simply by creatively expressing your heart and soul.

Journal

Journaling is a time-honored exercise that many people find to be very insightful and therapeutic. Simply writing your thoughts on paper or typing and saving them on the computer is a great way to express your deepest emotions, frustrations, joys, disappointments, and accomplishments. Most journals are kept private, and therefore provide a great outlet for expressing things that you might never say aloud to another person.

When dealing with the gut-wrenching, raw emotions of grief, expressing those emotions in written words can be very helpful, even if nobody but you will ever see them. It can also be a great way to measure your own growth and mark your journey. When you get five years down the road in your grief journey, looking back at your earlier journal entries can help you understand much more about yourself and see how you have grown through the process.

Write Poetry

If you are gifted in this area, poetry can be a great way to express the emotions you are experiencing in your grief. Poetry connects with people's souls in ways that no other form of literature does. If you are willing to share your poems with others, you could even become part of someone else's healing process.

Write a Book

David Saltzman died of Hodgkin's disease in 1990. He was twenty-two years old.[3] During his senior year at Yale University, he wrote and illustrated a book called *The Jester Has Lost His Jingle.*[4] Here is an excerpt from the book's liner notes.

> In this charming tale, the Jester awakes one morning to find laughter missing in his kingdom and he and his helpmate, Pharley, set off on a quest to find it. They ultimately discover that not only can laughter redeem a weary world, it also can provide the best tonic for anyone facing seemingly insurmountable obstacles.[5]

His tireless search for laughter brings the Jester to a hospital in the city, to the room of a little girl who has a tumor. The Jester helps the little girl find her laughter again, and soon the laughter spreads all the way back to the kingdom.

Because Saltzman died before his book could be published, his parents mortgaged their home to come up with the money to start their own publishing company and publish their son's book. Since then, the Jester has touched the lives of countless sick children, and helped them once again find their laughter, just like the girl in the book.

Kelsey Wood never lost her laughter during her five and a half year battle with cancer. She maintained an upbeat and positive attitude, and was a source of inspiration and strength for her family and friends. Her father, John, describes the day Kelsey died.

> The Wood family blinked one evening and experienced life screaming like a freight train; barreling through our tiny apartment with its whistle at full blast demolishing everything in its pathway leaving only a small piece of what was left of the life we had known.[6]

Kelsey's death left a huge hole in John's heart and a huge scar on his soul. He struggled with his faith. He struggled with his marriage. He struggled with his career. But rather than let all those struggles bring only negative results in his life, John decided to do something positive. He put all those struggles on paper. He did not sugar-coat anything. He bared his soul.

The result of John's decision to share the depth of his emotional and spiritual struggles is a book entitled *Life and Other Lies: Finding Meaning in Loss*[7]. Not only did the book provide a therapeutic outlet for John, through it he has provided a tool for therapeutic healing for others who find themselves on the lonely road of grief.

Write a Song

Karen Taylor-Good is a Grammy-nominated and highly-awarded singer-songwriter from Nashville. She is the creative force behind songs such as "How Can I Help You Say Goodbye" recorded by Patty Loveless, and "Not That Different" recorded by Collin Raye.[8]

When her nephew Paul died at age twenty-one, Karen sat down to write a song in his honor.[9] The result was a beautifully inspiring song entitled "Precious Child," which she first performed in Nashville at the 1998 National Conference of The Compassionate Friends, a national nonprofit self-help support organization that offers friendship and understanding to bereaved parents, grandparents and siblings.

I first became aware of "Precious Child" while Ashley was still alive. I was doing research into The Compassionate Friends and other support organizations for my Cancer Kids website project. The Compassionate Friends had adopted Karen's song and made it available on CD through their online store. I ordered a copy for myself, and began spreading the word about this hauntingly beautiful song.

When Ashley died, we played the song at her funeral as photos from her life were projected onto screens at the front of the auditorium. Numerous times during the months following Ashley's death, we would find Justin sitting alone in his room listening to "Precious Child" through headphones attached to his portable CD player. It was one of his special ways of remembering his big sister.

Because Karen chose to creatively share her grief through her gift of song, countless thousands of grieving parents, grandparents, siblings and other family members have been touched deeply and have found a powerful musical release for their own emotions during their time of loss.

Start a Foundation

Clayton Dabney was a very special little boy. He was intelligent, compassionate, and mature beyond his years. While still very young, he was diagnosed with rhabdomyosarcoma, a muscle tissue cancer.[10] Even when he was sick, he would share his toys with other sick children in the hospital.[11] At age six, Clayton's cancer took his precious little life.[12]

Clayton's parents, Scott and Shelby, did not want Clayton's spirit to die with him, so they created the Clayton Dabney Foundation for Kids with Cancer.[13] In the spirit of giving that was such a part of who Clayton was, the foundation helps provide "Everlasting Memories" for children in the last stages of cancer and their families.[14]

Our family has been personally blessed by this wonderful organization. When they found out that Ashley had been selected as an Olympic torchbearer for the 2002 Olympic Winter Games, and that she might not get to participate in the torch relay because she was so sick, the Clayton Dabney Foundation shifted into high gear. They arranged for Olympic gold medalist Nikki Stone to fly from Salt Lake City, Utah to Dallas,

Texas, and then drive from Dallas to Waxahachie to visit Ashley in our home.

Nikki was America's first-ever Olympic champion in the sport of inverted aerial skiing, winning the gold medal at the 1998 Olympic Winter Games in Nagano, Japan.[15] Her road to gold is quite an inspiring story.

To help you grasp the scope and impact of Nikki's visit, here is an article that Neal White, editor of the local newspaper and a dear family friend, published the day after the visit.

Real Hero

Gold medalist delivers Olympic torch to Ashley O'Rear, praises Waxahachie teen for being inspiration to others

By Neal White
Daily Light Editor

Representatives of the U.S. Olympic Committee traveled to Waxahachie on Monday to honor an Olympic torchbearer. Fourteen-year-old Ashley O'Rear was presented with the first Olympic torch that will be used to help carry the Olympic flame to the 2002 winter games in Salt Lake City. The torch was presented to Ashley by 1998 Olympic free style gold medalist Nikki Stone. Stone's visit to Waxahachie was arranged by the Clayton Dabney Foundation benefitting children with cancer.

The U.S. Olympic Committee selected Ashley to be an official torchbearer in October for her courage and inspiration to others.

She will carry the Olympic flame as it passes through Dallas on Dec. 12.

Lying on the sofa with her eyes closed, Ashley motioned with her left arm for her mom to come closer. "What is it?" Susan asked, as Ashley asked to sit up, struggling to enunciate the words above a whisper. "Are you hungry?" Susan asked, as she helped her daughter move into an upright position. Her face swollen from the tumor growing in her brain, Ashley nodded as her mom brought over a bowl of macaroni and cheese. After a few bites, Ashley motioned with her arm she was done just as the doorbell rang.

"That must be them," Susan said, wiping Ashley's face with a napkin before answering the door. Ashley's face brightened as Nikki Stone walked into the room. "I've been wanting to meet you," Stone said, sitting down on the sofa next to Ashley. "You're a true fighter. I just want you to know that you're my hero." Struggling to keep her eyes open, Ashley smiled as Stone talked.

"I've got something for you," she said, handing Ashley an official U.S. Olympic pin, an autographed copy of her book and a video of her 1998 competition at the Olympic winter games in Nagano, Japan. "I like to ski," Ashley said, working hard to get the words to form clearly. "I can ski really well because I have the little skis," she said, asking her mom to bring in her skis to show her guest.

"I also brought something else to show you," Stone said, reaching into her bag and pulling out a small box. "This is pretty special and I don't let very many people see it. But you're a pretty special person," Stone said, opening the box and pulling out her Olympic gold medal. "Go ahead, you can touch it," Stone said, as Ashley reached up and felt the engraving along the edge of the medal. "Here, let me help you," she said, holding Ashley's hand up and placing the medal in it. "It's pretty heavy, isn't it? I just want you to know that you've won your own medal for being as strong as you are and as brave as you are," Stone said. "Being an Olympic medalist is very difficult, but so is what you're doing."

Carrying Ashley's torch, Scott and Shelby Dabney handed it to Susan, who placed it into Ashley's arms. "I want you to know that this is the first Olympic torch that has been delivered for the winter games," Dabney said.

The couple created the foundation in honor of their son Clayton, who died six years ago from cancer. The Dabneys spend much of their time raising funds to assist other children with cancer, and arranging visits like the one with Ashley and Stone.

"This is a pretty special honor because you're a very special person," Stone added. "Not everyone gets to carry the Olympic flame. A lot of people were nominated, but only a few were selected. There are a lot of people who look up to you because of how strong you are. You give them hope."

For the next few minutes, Ashley listened intently as Stone told her what it was like being in the Olympics, the smile never once leaving Ashley's face. With the help of Susan, the two exchanged autographed photos of each other. "This means a lot to me," Stone said, carefully taking Ashley's photo and placing it in her bag.

Again at Ashley's request, Susan brought in the skis to show everyone. Passing them around for Stone to look at, Ashley's dad Paul shared how much his daughter loves being on the slopes. "In fact, she got sick the first time when we were on a ski trip in 1997 with our church youth group in Colorado," Paul explained. "Although she was sick, it didn't stop her from wanting to go back up the slopes. We knew she didn't feel good, but she insisted on going down for another run. When we got home and took her to the doctor, that was when we found out she had the first tumor," he said.

Following several surgeries to remove the tumor, along with chemotherapy and radiation treatments, Ashley's cancer went into remission, and Ashley continued on with her life — including participating in the family's annual ski trips. In September, she began having trouble with her balance and vision, prompting another trip to Children's Hospital in Dallas where an MRI revealed the tumor had returned. It has since spread to other parts of her body. A recent bout with congestion has left her weak, making it difficult for her to talk.

Motioning to her mom, Ashley asked to look at the videotape, and Paul gladly cued up the VCR. "There's my jump," Stone said, as she and Ashley watched the television screen. "You were up pretty high," Ashley said, amazed at the aerobatic maneuvers.

Although her body was weak, Ashley remained alert and focused as she began talking, forcing everyone to lean closer to hear her words. Susan was the first to understand as she started laughing. "She wants Justin (Ashley's younger brother) to be careful with her torch," Susan said, as everyone started to laugh. "I've got to carry that," Ashley smiled.

And while appreciative of the Dabneys for bringing the torch, Mr. Dabney wasn't spared from Ashley's good-natured ribbing for being a UT [University of Texas] grad. A dedicated Texas A&M fan, she couldn't understand why such a nice man would ever want to go to UT. Dabney enjoyed the ribbing.

"She's a fighter and an inspiration to others," he said. "Yes, she is," Paul agreed. "Yes, she is."

As Ashley and Stone continued to visit, Ashley never once tired of talking about skiing. When asked about winning the Olympic gold medal, Stone said it was one of the most amazing moments of her life. "The second most amazing moment is right now," she said. "It means a lot to me to be here and meet a girl who is a real hero."[16]

Ashley with Waxahachie Daily Light editor Neal White

Nikki told me later that when she got back home to Utah, she put Ashley's autographed picture on her refrigerator and looked at it every day because Ashley is such an inspiration to her.

Five days after Nikki's visit, Ashley died. "Everlasting Memories" is an appropriate name for what the Clayton Dabney Foundation is creating in the lives of families whose children are dying with cancer. If Scott and Shelby Dabney had not chosen to respond to their own grief by helping others, we would never have experienced the joy of meeting Nikki, or of Ashley being presented with the first 2002 Olympic torch. Because the Dabneys did choose to start the Clayton Dabney Foundation in memory of their precious son, we will always have some pretty amazing memories of Ashley's final days.

The Gregg Pearson Foundation was founded in 2008 as a response to a family tragedy.[17] At age 25, Gregg started having seizures. Eventually he was diagnosed with an inoperable brain tumor. He went through eleven years of treatments, including chemotherapy, radiation, and seizure medication. He underwent a new type of brain surgery in 2000 in an attempt to remove the tumor. The surgery was only partially successful, leaving about a third of the tumor in his brain. His condition deteriorated over the next couple of years, and Gregg died on Easter Sunday, April 20, 2003.[18]

Gregg's family started the Gregg Pearson Foundation to honor his legacy of caring for others. Since its inception, the foundation has provided financial, spiritual, and emotional support to families and friends who are dealing with cancer and other acute illnesses.[19]

The Jester Has Lost His Jingle, which is now available in a bilingual English/Spanish edition, has inspired the creation of the non-profit Jester & Pharley Phund, whose mission is to continue providing copies of *The Jester* to children with cancer and to boost literacy. Through 2012, more than 155,000 copies of *The Jester Has Lost His Jingle* and the Jester & Pharley Doll have been donated to sick children and in support of literacy. Through Phund Read-A-Thons, students donate the book and doll to children with cancer in their community.

Start a Movement

Rachel Scott was the first student killed in the horrific attack on Columbine High School in Columbine, Colorado, on April 20, 1999. Before the day was over, twelve students and one teacher had been murdered in cold blood, and the two perpetrators—also students at Columbine—had taken their own lives in a final act of cowardly desperation.

Rachel's brother Craig witnessed the killing of two of his friends that day. The three of them were sitting at a table in the library, studying, when the two gunmen entered and opened fire. His two friends were killed, but Craig's life was spared when the killers became distracted just as they were raising their guns to shoot him. Craig walked out of school that day covered in the blood of his two friends, only to learn that his sister Rachel had been killed as well.

Just a month before Rachel died, she wrote an essay for one of her high school classes. The essay was entitled, "My Ethics, My Codes of Life." In it she talked about the importance of being honest and compassionate, and of always looking for the best and beauty in others. She defined compassion as "forgiving, loving, helping, leading, and showing mercy for others." Then she wrote something that would forever change the lives of her family, and of millions of people all over the world who would come to know Rachel's story.

> I have this theory that if one person can go out of their way to show compassion, then it will start a chain reaction of the same. People will never know how far a little kindness can go.

Rachel challenged others to test her codes of trust, compassion and beauty, and finished by writing, "You just may start a chain reaction."

With Rachel's message ringing in his ears, her father Darrell began speaking to anyone who would listen. He used Rachel's writings and drawings to spread her message of compassion and kindness, and to convince people that these qualities, when practiced by more and more people, could start a chain reaction that would impact every layer of society. Out of this effort was born the non-profit organization Rachel's Challenge.

Rachel's Challenge speakers travel all over the country—and the world—telling Rachel's story and challenging school students and corporate executives alike to start their own chain reactions of kindness. Each year, more than two million people are touched by Rachel's message of compassion.

Because Rachel's family chose to honor her legacy with Rachel's Challenge, millions of people all over the world have accepted the challenge to start a chain reaction of kindness by showing compassion to those around them.[20]

Miscellaneous Ideas

Here are a few additional ideas for ways you can channel your grief in very positive ways. Use your own imagination to come up with your own ideas.

- Make a quilt (or have one made) from some of your deceased loved one's t-shirts. Ann, a dear friend at church, made just such a quilt for Justin from Ashley's t-shirts. It is an amazing thing of beauty! Someday Justin will be able to use the quilt to tell his children all about his beautiful sister and all the things she loved to do, as represented by the t-shirts in the quilt.

- Plant a tree in memory of your loved one. Ashley's classmates raised money and planted a live oak tree in the front yard of Waxahachie Junior High, the last school where Ashley attended for an entire school year. They also had a marble bench placed in front of the tree with the inscription, "In Loving Memory of Ashley O'Rear." Later, they raised more money and purchased fourteen crape myrtle trees which were planted all around the Junior High.

- Express your grief through art. You might even turn your art into products—t-shirts, coffee mugs, greeting cards, posters, calendars, etc.— that you can sell to fund other grief-related projects. Google the phrase "make t-shirts and gifts online" and you should find several sources for creating your own online shop and selling merchandise with your own artwork.

- Volunteer at a local hospital or children's hospital. As a volunteer, you can bring comfort and compassion and happiness to other families who are struggling.

- Provide toys and prizes to a children's hospital. Children's Medical Center's Hematology and Oncology Clinic—where Ashley went for her check-ups—always had a rather significant stash of prizes and toys for the kids who came into the clinic. Check with your nearest children's hospital and see what kinds of toys and prizes they could use.

- Start a grief recovery group.

- Create a website. It might be a memorial website honoring your deceased loved one, a website dedicated to information about a certain disease, a website dedicated to helping others with their grief journey, or even a blog chronicling your own grief journey.

- Participate in memorial events, such as The Compassionate Friends' annual Worldwide Candle Lighting.

Look for the Good

We've all heard the question before. Maybe you've even asked the question yourself. It's a difficult question, to be sure, often creating a spiritual dilemma in the mind and heart of the one asking. "Why do bad things happen to good people?"

The reasoning goes something like this. "If God is all-powerful, and if God is compassionate and loves everyone, how could such an all-powerful, loving God allow bad things to happen to the people who are striving every day to serve Him?" On the surface, this does seem to pose a dilemma. But this question is usually not asked on the surface. It generally emerges from the emotional depths of a hurting person's very soul. "Why, God? Why?"

Let's look at four examples that will help us understand why bad things sometimes happen to good people.

David

God had been watching David from the time he was a young shepherd boy tending his father's sheep. Even though he was the youngest of Jesse's eight sons, and even though he was not voted by his peers as most likely to be the next king of Israel, God saw something in this shepherd boy that many overlooked. God saw David's heart.

In Acts 13:22, we are told that God considered David to be a man after his own heart. God's assessment of David was that David was a good man. This makes the story in 2 Samuel 11 even more tragic, because it's not the kind of thing you would expect from a man after God's own heart.

King David lusted after beautiful Bathsheba, sent messengers to bring her to his bedroom, and had sex with her. Here we find a good man—David—committing a disgusting sin—adultery. This little indiscretion on David's part resulted in an unplanned pregnancy for Bathsheba. Suddenly, the man after God's own heart found himself in quite a pickle.

Because David—the king and leader of God's people—had shown complete disregard for God's laws through his sinful actions, God told David that his and Bathsheba's newborn son would die. When the child became ill, David wept bitterly for seven days and begged God to spare his son's life. On the seventh day, the baby boy died.

> Sometimes bad things happen to good people
> as a result of their own sins and mistakes.

John is a good man, dedicated to his family, faithful to his wife. He is a deacon in his local church and participates in many community volunteer activities as a member of his local Kiwanis club. He is genuinely a good man.

Lately he has been struggling with minor depression because of the financial strains on his family. One evening he stops by the convenience store on his way home from work and picks up a six-pack of beer—something totally out of character for him—as a way to try to deal with the depression. When he arrives home and sits down at his desk to pay bills, his frustration level climbs and those feelings of depression begin to close in on him. Before he even realizes it, he has consumed three cans of beer.

When it comes time for the family to head across town for dinner at the home of some dear friends, John makes his way out to the car before everyone else, hoping that his family won't see him staggering and stumbling and won't realize that he is drunk. With everyone loaded in the car, John backs out of the driveway. In his inebriated condition, he does not notice the speeding car coming way too fast down their residential street. John backs out of the driveway right in front of the speeding car. The full force of the impact is focused on the driver's side back door, where John's youngest daughter Abby is sitting. Abby is killed instantly.

John is devastated. A week after the funeral, his wife files for divorce. His whole world is falling apart, all as a result of one bad decision. Sometimes bad things happen to good people as a result of their own sins and mistakes.

Uriah

Uriah was a good man. He was a good soldier, faithful to his king. He was a good husband, faithful to his beautiful wife Bathsheba. Every indication is that he was a man of valor and integrity. He was genuinely a good man.

The Israelite army was at war. They had already engaged in several successful military campaigns and were pressing forward. Uriah and his buddies were destroying the enemies of God. This was not some meaningless war. They were fighting for everything they believed in.

One day Uriah received a strange message from his commander Joab. "The king wants to see you. Return to Jerusalem immediately." "The king wants to see me? How does he even know who I am? What would he possibly want with me?" Faithful subject that he was, Uriah set out for Jerusalem and appeared before King David.

David asked Uriah a series of strange questions. "How is Joab? How are the soldiers? How is the war progressing?" These were not strange questions in and of themselves, but didn't the king already have people who kept him informed on matters concerning the war? Why would he pull a common soldier out of the middle of the fighting to ask him these questions? It just did not make sense.

Uriah obviously did not have a clue that the king for whom he fought bravely had slept with his wife whom he loved deeply. He did not know that his beautiful wife was now pregnant with the king's child. Nor did he realize that he had become nothing more than an expendable pawn in a selfish king's pathetic game of self-preservation.

As he returned to the battle, he unwittingly carried his own death warrant and delivered it into the hands of his reluctant executioner, his commander Joab. Once again Uriah picked up the sword and engaged in battle. Once again he faithfully served the very king who was about to have him brutally murdered. Once again he faithfully served his God.

It was in the middle of this valiant struggle against God's enemies that Uriah met his unfortunate demise. He was not, however, simply a casualty of war. Rather, he was the victim of cold-blooded murder. Upon orders from the king, Joab commanded the men who were fighting with Uriah to abandon him during the heat of the battle. The faithful soldiers, themselves merely pawns in the king's game, simply followed orders. Uriah was killed. However, he did not die as a result of his own sins or mistakes. Uriah died as a result of King David's sinful actions.

> Sometimes bad things happen to good people
> as a result of someone else's sins and mistakes.

Jill is a beautiful young Christian woman attending a Christian university. Though she is very attractive, she has always made it a priority to dress modestly. She is even working on developing a line of modest clothing for Christian teenagers and young adults. She is studying Marketing in college to prepare herself for launching her line of modest clothing.

One Wednesday after attending midweek prayer service at her church, Jill arrives back at her apartment. She changes into her pajamas and pours herself a glass of cold milk to enjoy while working on her homework. As she walks out of the kitchen, an intruder grabs her from behind and puts his hand over her mouth so she cannot scream. He drags her back to her bedroom, covers her mouth with duct tape and brutally rapes her.

When the rapist finally leaves, Jill removes the duct tape and calls 9-1-1. She is taken to the local hospital and put through a series of tests and procedures. After what seems like an eternity, she is finally released from the hospital and taken back to her apartment by two police officers.

For the next several nights she is terrified to go into her apartment alone, and arranges for one of her football player friends to go in first and make sure no one is inside. She has difficulty going to sleep, because she is afraid that someone might break in during the night and rape her again. When she does finally doze off, her peaceful sleep is interrupted by horrific nightmares that cause her to bolt awake sweating and screaming. After a week of this, she simply cannot take any more. She drops out of college and moves back home with her parents.

Jill did nothing wrong, yet her life has been completely turned upside down and her lifelong dreams derailed. Sometimes bad things happen to good people as a result of someone else's sins or mistakes.

Job

Any time I start feeling sorry for myself and thinking that life is unfair, I like to remind myself of the story of Job in the Old Testament. It helps me keep things in perspective. Job was a good man, "blameless and upright; he feared God and shunned evil" (Job 1:1 NIV). In fact, Job was such a good man that God bragged about him to Satan.

One day as Job was going about his daily tasks, within a few minutes' time four different servants arrived to tell him that all of his livestock had been either killed or stolen, all of his servants had been killed—except those who escaped to bring word to Job—and finally all ten of his children had been killed in a freak accident.

Can you imagine? Within a few minutes Job's world had completely fallen apart! He was devastated.

Sometime after all of these tragic events, Job began to break out in sores. They were nasty, painful sores that ended up covering his entire body from head to toe. He used a piece of broken pottery to scrape the sores, trying to get at least a little bit of relief.

Then his friends showed up. However, I don't know that "friends" is exactly the best description of Eliphaz, Bildad, and Zophar. In a situation of deep grief and physical suffering like Job's, most friends would try to comfort you in your distress. Not these guys. They proceeded to explain to Job that he must have done something terribly wrong and sinful in order for all of these bad things to be happening to him.

But his friends were wrong! Unlike King David, Job's suffering was not the result of his own sins and mistakes. Nor was it the result of someone else's sins and mistakes, as was the case with Uriah. All these bad things happened to Job because Satan was trying to get into Job's head, trying to get Job to turn his back on God.

> *Sometimes bad things happen to good people because Satan is hard at work, tempting them and trying to get them to turn away from God.*

This certainly fits the description that Peter gave us of Satan. "Your enemy the devil prowls around like a roaring lion looking for someone to devour" (1 Peter 5:8 NIV).

Misfortune

On Sunday, December 26, 2004, at 7:58 a.m. local Sumatran time, a 9.1 magnitude earthquake occurred off of the western coast of northern Indonesia. The epicenter was located 155 miles south southeast of the city of Banda Aceh, Sumatra, Indonesia, at a depth of 18.6 miles.[1] The death toll from this massive earthquake and the tsunami that it spawned has been estimated at nearly 230,000 people.[2]

On Friday, March 11, 2011, at 2:46 p.m. local Japanese time, a 9.0 magnitude earthquake occurred off of the eastern coast of Japan. The epicenter was located eighty miles east of Sendai, Honshu, Japan, at a depth of 18.6 miles.[3] The tsunami waves spawned by this earthquake reached a maximum height, at landfall, of over 97 feet. More than 15,000 people were killed.[4]

Between April 25 and April 28, 2011, a "super outbreak" of tornadoes ravaged the Southern, Midwestern and Northeastern United States. A total of 388 tornadoes spread across twenty-one states and even into Canada.[5,6] Approximately 339 people lost their lives, making this the fourth deadliest tornado outbreak in United States history.[7]

Steve Irwin was known to people all over the world as the Crocodile Hunter. He spent his life catching, observing, and teaching people about all kinds of animals. On September 4, 2006, while filming a series of underwater shots for an upcoming film, Irwin was attacked by a stingray. The ray thrust its barbed tail through Irwin's chest and into his heart. He died of cardiac arrest.[8]

What about all these people who have died as the result of a storm or natural disaster? What about people, like Steve Irwin, who have been killed by wild animals? What about the hundreds of thousands of people who die each year from cancer, or even something as seemingly innocuous as the seasonal flu? Sometimes bad things happen to good people not because of anything they have done wrong, not because of someone else's sins or misdeeds, and not necessarily because Satan has specifically targeted them.

> Sometimes bad things happen to good people simply because they happen to be in the wrong place at the wrong time; or simply as the result of natural events or disasters, accidents, illness or disease.

We must remember that God did not create this world to be permanent or perfect. Our permanent, perfect home is heaven. God purposely created a flawed, imperfect world—though stunningly beautiful—and then set the laws of nature in motion to govern the everyday happenings in this world. Sometimes man's course collides with nature's course, and people end up getting hurt or killed in the process.

A Healthy Perspective on Suffering

In Luke 13, Jesus was trying to help his followers understand some of these difficult concepts related to human suffering. Someone brought to his attention the horrific act of Pilate, who had mixed the blood of some Galileans with their own sacrifices. In the course of this conversation, Jesus posed a very thought-provoking question. "Do you think that these Galileans were worse sinners than all the other Galileans because they suffered this way?" His answer was an emphatic, "No!"

Then Jesus brought up another incident that involved human suffering and death. "Or those eighteen who died when the tower in Siloam fell on them—do you think they were more guilty than all the others living in Jerusalem?" Again, his emphatic answer was, "No!"

I have conversed with people in the past who firmly believe the cliché, "Everything happens for a reason." Their conclusion then, when something bad happens in the life of a Christian, is that God must be punishing that person for something bad that he or she has done; or that God is orchestrating the events of that person's life in order to teach him or her some kind of important lesson.

We have already seen, from Job's situation, that this kind of thinking on the part of Job's friends was faulty. Job was not being punished for some wrongdoing. Jesus echoes that truth here in Luke 13. There was no correlation between the bad things that happened to these people and some sin or wrongdoing in their lives. Do not be fooled by the faulty thinking of Job's friends. Do not allow yourself to be sucked into the never-ending quicksand of trying to figure out the reason behind every little thing—or even every big thing— that happens in your life. All you will end up doing is driving yourself crazy!

Digging Deeper

There is another principle that comes into play when we try to understand how human suffering can exist in the presence of God's mercy. I'm not sure if this should be considered a fifth reason why bad things happen to good people, alongside the four reasons already discussed, or if this is more like an umbrella principle that applies to all four of those reasons. Either way, it's something we must consider.

The apostle Paul had a "thorn in the flesh" that caused him great torment (2 Corinthians 12:6-10). Scholars have speculated for centuries as to the exact nature of Paul's thorn, with no consensus. But that doesn't really matter. What is important is the principle.

Whatever was causing Paul's torment, he pleaded with God three times to remove it. Three times God's answer was, "No." Why? "My grace is sufficient for you, for my power is made perfect in weakness." Let that sink in.

Jesus and his disciples were walking along in John 9 when they came upon a blind man. This man was well-known in the neighborhood because he sat and begged day after day. He had been blind since birth, which prompted a question from Jesus' disciples. "Who sinned, this man or his parents, that he was born blind?"

Jesus' answer shouldn't surprise us, based on the things we learned from Job's friends; and based on Jesus' answer to the previous questions from his disciples about the Galileans and those in Siloam who experienced suffering. "Neither this man nor his parents sinned," Jesus said.

What may come as a surprise is the statement Jesus made next. "This happened so that the work of God might be displayed in his life." We don't know how old the blind man was, but we do know that he had been blind his entire life. He had never seen a sunset, had never enjoyed the bright colors of fall foliage, and didn't even know what his mother's face looked like—all things that we take for granted. He had never been able to hold a job, reduced instead to the humiliation of sitting in public places begging for sustenance from those who passed by. No doubt he had prayed for God to heal his blindness, and until now God's answer had always been, "No."

The Israelites lived as slaves in the land of Egypt for over four hundred years. According to Exodus 1, the Egyptian taskmasters oppressed the Israelites with forced labor, worked them ruthlessly, and made their lives bitter. It was a cruel, harsh existence, and it lasted more than four hundred years. Many Israelites were born into slavery, lived their entire lives in slavery, and died in slavery. For them, there was literally no end to their oppression.

One has to imagine that there were thousands upon thousands of prayers lifted to God during those four hundred years, begging him to put an end to the suffering, pleading with him to show his power to the heathen Egyptians by bringing them down and raising up his own people to prominence and power. Actually, we do not have to imagine that those prayers were offered. God himself tells us they were.

When God appeared to Moses in the burning bush in Exodus 3 and commissioned Moses to go into Egypt and demand that Pharaoh release his people, he told Moses, "I have indeed seen the misery of my people in Egypt. I have heard them crying out because of their slave drivers, and I am concerned about their suffering. So I have come down to rescue them from the hand of the Egyptians and to bring them up out of that land into a good and spacious land, a land flowing with milk and honey." (Exodus 3:7-8 NIV)

We cannot escape the question, because at some point someone either has already asked it or will ask it. "Really, God? For four hundred years your people cried out to you and you ignored their plea for help. For four hundred years you watched them suffer and you did nothing. And now, all of a sudden, after four hundred years, *now* you've heard their cry and are concerned about their suffering? *Now* you're ready to rescue them? Really?"

It's a valid question. Why would God allow his people to suffer the atrocities of Egyptian bondage for such a long period of time and seemingly turn a deaf ear to their cries for deliverance?

Why would God allow that poor man in John 9 to be born blind and live his whole life in darkness, never experiencing the joy of sight that most people take for granted?

Why would he not remove Paul's thorn in the flesh? Paul was arguably one of the most faithful and effective servants of God who ever lived, devoting his entire life to traveling from place to place, preaching the gospel, and establishing congregations of the Lord's church. James tells us that "The prayer of a righteous person is powerful and effective" (James 5:16 NKJV). You could make a pretty convincing argument that Paul was a righteous man. So why would God not grant Paul's request?

Here is the principle that I believe is at work in every one of these situations. God has a master plan. He is always looking at the big picture. We have a tendency to be spiritually myopic and focus only on our little bitty piece of that big picture. It may be that what I want in any situation is not what fits best in God's big picture, his master plan.

When we look back at the Israelites' situation in Egypt from our vantage point a few thousand years down the road, it is easy to see how that whole situation was part of God's master plan. But if I had been one of those Israelites who had been born into slavery and had lived my whole life in slavery, it would be much more difficult for me to see or appreciate the big picture.

The reason the man in John 9 had been born blind, according to Jesus, was so that the work of God could be shown in his life. The reason God did not remove Paul's thorn in the flesh was because God's power is made perfect in our weakness.

Sometimes, God can accomplish more through us in our suffering than in our comfort. Sometimes, my weakness is a necessary conduit through which his power can be more mightily seen and understood. Sometimes, the simple truth is that my suffering allows his work to be seen in my life much more clearly than if I did not suffer. It may even be that my suffering is needed in order for his master plan to be accomplished, in order for his big picture to be complete.

I don't necessarily like these truths, and they may not be what I would choose if I had my druthers. But being a Christian means submitting my will to God's. It means accepting his will for my life, regardless of what his will is or whether I like it. It means looking at life from an eternal perspective, because only through that prism does the reality of human suffering in the presence of God's mercy make any sense.

Shedding Some Light

Jesus told an interesting parable that I believe can shed some light on this whole problem of human suffering.

> Jesus told them another parable: "The kingdom of heaven is like a man who sowed good seed in his field. But while everyone was sleeping, his enemy came and sowed weeds among

145

the wheat, and went away. When the wheat sprouted and formed heads, then the weeds also appeared.

"The owner's servants came to him and said, 'Sir, didn't you sow good seed in your field? Where then did the weeds come from?'

"'An enemy did this,' he replied.

"The servants asked him, 'Do you want us to go and pull them up?'

"'No,' he answered, 'because while you are pulling the weeds, you may root up the wheat with them. Let both grow together until the harvest. At that time I will tell the harvesters: First collect the weeds and tie them in bundles to be burned; then gather the wheat and bring it into my barn.'"

Matthew 13:24–30 (NIV)

I believe there is a simple message in this parable. God is not going to take away all the bad stuff from our lives. He is going to leave it there to grow right along with the good stuff. He is not going to take away all the bad people, either. As we go through this life, there is going to be good stuff and there is going to be bad stuff. There are going to be good people and there are going to be bad people. God's message to us is, "Just hang on, and I will sort it all out at the Harvest."

So, if it is a given that we are going to experience suffering in this life, how do we keep a healthy perspective on it all? I believe there are two things we need to remember that will help us keep suffering in perspective, and they both come straight from Scripture.

It Gets Better

Remember the comforting message of that old gospel hymn? "This world is not my home, I'm just a-passin' through. My treasures are laid up somewhere beyond the blue." That's more than just a gospel hymn. It's biblical truth.

> But our citizenship is in heaven. And we eagerly await a Savior from there, the Lord Jesus Christ, who, by the power that enables him to bring everything under his control, will transform our lowly bodies so that they will be like his glorious body.
>
> Philippians 3:20–21 (NIV)

I love being an American, and I love being a Texan. But in the grand scheme of things, my U.S. citizenship is not what's really important, nor does my citizenship in the Great State of Texas amount to much more than a hill of beans. My true citizenship is in heaven. My journey through this life is just that—a journey. In the words of another old gospel hymn, "I am a poor wayfaring stranger." I am merely a sojourner here in this world.

This is not all there is. No matter how bad things get down here, no matter how unfair life can be, no matter how wicked the world around me becomes, there is something much better waiting for me. I just have to keep holding on to God, knowing that it will all be worth it someday.

The greatest goal of any Christian parent is to help their children get to heaven. Ashley has made it! She is exactly where I want to be. I just need to hold on to the words of King David when his son died. "Can I bring him back again? I will go to him, but he will not return to me" (2 Samuel 12:23 NIV). I know that I will see Ashley again, because she has already arrived at our mutual destination. I cannot bring her back to me, but I can go see her.

My citizenship is in heaven. That amazing truth will help me make it through whatever manner of darkness and suffering life can possibly throw at me.

It's All Good

There is a verse in Romans that has become my motto for life. The apostle Paul wrote, "And we know that all things work together for good to those who love God" (Romans 8:28 NKJV).

This is an amazing promise. But it is just as important to notice what God did not promise here, as it is to notice what he did promise. God never promised us that, if we believe in him, nothing bad will ever happen to us. The promise does not say, "Only good things will happen to those who love God." This is an important concept for Christians to understand.

What God did promise us is that all things will work together for good to those who love him. Bad things are going to happen, even to good people. We have already seen a number of reasons why this is true. God's powerful promise to you is that he can make something good come out of even the bad stuff in your life. In fact, he promised you that *everything* that happens to you in your life—the good stuff and the bad stuff—will all work together to produce good results. I don't know about you, but that gives me a whole lot of peace and comfort.

Real Promise or Empty Promise?

Okay, so let's put it to the test. Ashley had cancer. She threw up for hours on end. She lost all of her beautiful blonde hair. She got so weak that she could not even walk or stand without assistance. She almost died several times because of the side effects of the medicines that were supposed to save her life. She spent hours and days and weeks and months confined to a hospital room, missing out on so much of the stuff that little girls are supposed to enjoy about life, missing out on so many "normal" activities that her friends got to enjoy.

Let me make this perfectly clear. Cancer is not good! There is *nothing* inherently good about cancer. It is a debilitating, deadly disease. It steals childhood. It steals life. It leaves parents with empty arms and broken hearts. It leaves little brothers struggling to even figure out what life is supposed to be like after cancer has stolen a big sister. In case you missed it the first time, I will shout it again. *There is nothing good about cancer!*

So the question is, "What good can possibly come from something as horribly bad as childhood cancer?"

Remember that we are testing a promise here, and that the promise is conditional. It is for those who love the Lord. Ashley was never embarrassed or ashamed to show her faith. She was never "in your face" about it, either; she simply allowed it to shine through in her life every day. You will remember that her motto for living was "Trust in God, and never give up." She was never afraid to tell people that God was her source of strength and comfort. Ashley loved God!

Shortly after I began posting updates about Ashley on the Internet and sending out updates by e-mail to people who wanted to keep up with her progress, I "met" a lady from California through e-mail. Her name is Woody. She would send an occasional e-mail encouraging Ashley and encouraging our family.

Then one day the e-mail I received from Woody caused my heart to drop. Woody had been to visit her doctor and before she left she was told that she had breast cancer. Obviously, she was devastated. My heart ached for this precious soul who had given so much of herself to encourage us, and now was faced with her own cancer battle. I continued reading.

Woody said that as she replayed the news over and over in her mind—"You have breast cancer"— and as she anticipated the frightening treatments and uncertainty that lay ahead of her, a thought crossed her mind that gave her great strength and comfort. Woody thought to herself, *If Ashley can do it, then so can I.* My heart leaped for joy when I read those words! Woody had found the strength and the courage to face her own nightmare because of Ashley's determination and unwavering faith.

In that moment my awareness of what God was doing mushroomed. Suddenly I realized that God had a plan for Ashley. Through Ashley's suffering—or to be more precise, through Ashley's faithfulness in the face of suffering—God was going to bless other people and help them with their own struggles. Perhaps it would be a few people; perhaps it would be countless thousands. The numbers did not matter. That was completely up to God. The cool thing was, because Ashley chose to remain faithful to God throughout her battle, God was going to use her to bless other people's lives! God was making good stuff come out of bad stuff, just like he promised.

Through the years I have lost count of the people who have e-mailed me, written to me, called me on the phone, or spoken to me in person to tell me how inspired they have been by Ashley's story, and how they have found renewed strength to face their own struggles because of the determination and faith with which she faced hers.

Numerous times I have had someone tell me, "I don't even know how I ended up on Ashley's web page, but I have spent the last three hours reading every word and bawling my eyes out. She was an amazing young lady!" It warms my heart every single time. It reminds me that Ashley had a purpose and fulfilled that purpose beautifully. God has caused much good to come into our lives and into the lives of countless other people because of Ashley's faithful stewardship of her cancer battle. God has certainly kept his promise in Romans 8:28.

Conclusion

No one ever said life was going to be easy. God never promised us a life free from tragedy, heartache, or grief. Bad things are going to happen, even to good people. That does not mean that God is not there, or that He does not care.

As you go through life and face the struggles that life puts in front of you; as you strive to make sense of your grief and climb back out of the pit of despair; I encourage you to just hang onto God for dear life. Continue loving him and looking to him to find your strength and comfort. And then start looking for the good, because it will be there in some form or fashion. That is a promise from God!

Someone Else's Grief

W atching another person grieve is difficult, especially if it is someone for whom you care deeply. You want so desperately to be able to do something to help, to take away their pain. You want to make sure you say the right thing, and that you do not say anything that will open up the wound and cause even more pain. What can I do? What should I say? What should I not say? How do I help my friend who is grieving?

If those are the questions that are on your mind, thank you for being such a caring, compassionate person. This chapter is written especially for you.

The Right Words

On the Saturday that Ashley died, that morning a large crowd of friends slowly began assembling at our house. To this day, I do not know exactly how or why that happened, but every time Susan or I walked out of our bedroom to get something from the front of the house, there were a few more people there, just sitting and visiting…waiting. Apparently word had spread that Ashley's condition was deteriorating, and these wonderful friends just wanted to be there for us.

Throughout the course of the day, I had conversations with numerous people, both before and after Ashley died. Here is what I find both interesting and enlightening about that whole situation. Out of all those conversations with dear friends at such a momentous time in our lives, I do not remember a single thing that anyone said to me that day, nor do I remember the specifics of any of the hundreds of conversations at the funeral home visitation on Monday evening, or at the funeral on Tuesday afternoon. There were probably at least a few people who had agonized greatly over what they would say when they spoke to Susan and Justin and me. Some had probably rehearsed in detail the exact words they would say, just to make sure they did not say the wrong thing. Ironically, all of that agonizing and all of that rehearsing was completely unnecessary, because I do not even remember anything they said!

What I do remember is the fact that there were a lot of people at our house that Saturday who just wanted to be near us because they loved us and they loved Ashley.

What I do remember is that we did not even have to think about little nagging things like doing the laundry or washing the dishes, because some of those dear friends took it upon themselves to do the things that they saw needed to be done, so that we would not have to worry about them.

What I do remember is that people stepped in to help explore funeral options, and took it upon themselves to do the legwork to make sure those arrangements were taken care of.

What I do remember is that literally hundreds of people showed up for visitation on Monday night, just to see Susan and Justin and me, to see Ashley as she lay in state, and to hug us and cry with us and share their memories of Ashley with us. They came to love us.

What I do remember is the compassionate manner in which the staff of the Waxahachie Civic Center worked with us to make sure that every detail of Ashley's funeral was a perfect tribute to the beauty of her life. And I remember, like it was yesterday, walking into the grand ballroom of the civic center for Ashley's funeral and seeing an endless sea of people—nearly 2,000 in all—who had come to share with us in the pain of our loss, and in the joy of remembering what an incredibly special person Ashley was. I remember sitting on the second row as people passed by the coffin to say their final goodbyes to Ashley. Many of them turned and mouthed the words *I love you* to us, blew us kisses, or simply looked at us through eyes of love and compassion, sharing in our brokenness. People loving us and just being there and doing little things…that is what I remember—not what people said.

There are no "right words" that you can speak to lighten the load of my grief. Nothing you can say will fill the hole in my heart, or take away my sadness. No matter how profound those words are, and no matter how many times you rehearse them in your head, they cannot take away my pain. *Nothing* can take away my pain, because hearts that are broken by grief simply cannot be fixed.

However, the love and support and genuine help that we received from our friends, church family, and physical family went a very long way in providing comfort and easing the burden of our pain. It's sort of like when you rub salve or ointment into a wound. It doesn't make the wound go away. It doesn't stop the pain. But it does provide a welcomed soothing sensation in the midst of the pain.

Please don't misunderstand what I am saying. When you visit someone who is grieving, words will obviously be exchanged. Clichés will probably be spoken. "It is comforting to know that she is in a better place," *which she is*. "She's not suffering anymore," *which she isn't*. As far as I am concerned, it is perfectly okay to make such statements. I was never offended by such a statement when Ashley died, and we heard many of them.

The whole point I am trying to make is that the words you speak will not be nearly as important—or nearly as powerful—as your simple presence. No words, no matter how profound, can provide relief from the pain of my grief. Love and friendship, however, provide a soothing comfort and reassurance in the midst of the pain. Don't try to come up with something really profound to say. You are wasting your time if you do, because most likely it will not be remembered anyway. Simply be yourself, say what is on your heart, and just be there and express your love and friendship.

The Wrong Words

In fact, the harder you try to come up with something really profound to say to a grieving person, the more likely you are to get yourself into trouble.

Clay and Connie are friends from church who also lost a child, Trent, to cancer. Trent was only five years old when he died. Clay told me that he realized, near the end of Trent's struggle, that Trent was not going to make it. He resigned himself to the fact that Trent was going to die. In essence, he had given up hope for Trent's survival.

The day before Trent died, many friends came by Clay and Connie's house to offer their love and support. One friend, in a conversation with Clay, said, "Well, if it was my child, I sure wouldn't give up hope." Several others who were nearby heard the comment and stepped in to whisk Clay away and then asked the other person to leave. That person could not possibly have known how he would have reacted if he had been in Clay and Connie's shoes. Such a statement was totally inappropriate and revealed a complete lack of concern for Clay and Connie's feelings.

There are no "right words" to speak to the person who is grieving. But there are certainly some wrong things to say. "I understand how you feel" is a statement that, though intended to soothe and comfort, often has the exact opposite effect. I have heard people express various degrees of negative reaction, including anger, to such a statement. I personally do not find such a statement to be blatantly offensive, but others do. And I think I can understand why.

There have been a number of instances when Susan and I have been asked to talk to other families who have lost a child. The person making the request usually makes a statement that goes something like this. "I think you can help them because you can understand their feelings." I will always welcome the opportunity to talk with another parent who has lost a child, because I am walking that road myself, and I understand the importance of fellow sojourners helping each other along the way. But I am very uneasy with the assumption that I know how anyone feels, just because our situations are similar.

I am not that other parent. Ashley is not the other family's child. Every person, every relationship, every situation is different. I try not to assume that I understand how anyone feels who has lost a child, because they may be experiencing feelings that I have not experienced. So the best I can offer is usually to simply listen. Just like no one else could have come up with the right words to ease my pain when Ashley died, I certainly do not have any magic words or secret formulas or profound advice that will take away another grieving parent's pain. I do, however, have a good set of ears, a broad set of shoulders, and a heart full of compassion. Those are infinitely more important than any "right words" could ever be.

Is It Okay to Talk About the Deceased?

Many people wonder if it is appropriate to talk about someone who has died to the people who are grieving that person's death. It would be terribly inconsistent of me to answer that question either "yes" or "no" and assume that my answer is the correct answer for every person who is grieving. Remember, one of the fundamental principles of this book is: "There is no universal, one-size-fits-all formula for grieving or grief management. No two people grieve in exactly the same way."

I will share with you my answer to that question. But please realize that this is only my answer. Another person who is grieving may not feel the same way, and that is perfectly okay.

Shortly after Ashley's death, I began putting together a web page that paid tribute to her life. On that web page, I have posted a brief poem that expresses beautifully my feelings, though I did not write the poem myself.

The Mention of Her Name

The mention of my Child's Name
May bring tears to my eyes,
But it never fails to bring
Music to my ears.
If you are really my Friend,
Let me hear the beautiful music of her name.
It soothes my broken heart
And sings to my soul.

—Anonymous

Susan and I are blessed that most of our friends and family are very comfortable talking about Ashley in our presence. We love to hear people share their memories of our precious daughter. Every once in a while, someone will run across a picture of Ashley among their family photos, make an extra copy of the picture, and give us the extra copy. Often, they will share with us their memories surrounding that picture. It brings joy to our hearts to know that people still remember Ashley, and that those memories are a source of joy for them.

Sometimes people are not comfortable talking to a grieving person about their deceased loved one. They may think, "I don't want to cause my friend any more pain by talking about the person they have lost." Again, I can only tell you how I feel, but you cannot possibly cause me pain when it comes to my losing Ashley. The pain is already there, has already been there, and will always be there. As the poem above suggests, the mention of Ashley's name may bring a tear to my eye, but that does not mean that you have caused me pain. Hearing people talk about Ashley is "music to my ears." "Let me hear the beautiful music of her name. It soothes my broken heart and sings to my soul."

I have heard numerous brokenhearted people agonize over the fact that some people seem to avoid mentioning their deceased loved one in their presence. Ashley was a physical presence on this earth and in our lives for fourteen years. She was our first child. She was our only daughter. For fourteen years the reality of our daily lives was filled with her presence. As already mentioned, you cannot cause me pain by talking about her. The pain of her absence is an ever-present reality in my life. You can cause me pain, however, by pretending that she never existed; by acting as though my fourteen years of beautiful memories are not worth talking about. I may shed a few tears as we talk about Ashley, but I am honored that you remember her, and that your memories are important enough that you want to share them with me.

Clay and Connie feel the same way. I had not yet met them when they lost their precious Trent. I remember my first conversation with Clay concerning their loss of Trent and our loss of Ashley. He made a comment that I found particularly insightful. It went something like this: "Parents love talking about their children. When a child takes his first steps, says his first word, makes a good grade in school, has a piano recital, gets chosen for the football team, or makes first chair in band, parents love to brag to others about their children's accomplishments. Trent is my child. He will always be my child. The only difference is that there will never again be any new things to talk about, because he is gone. But that doesn't make me want to talk about him any less than any other parent wants to talk about their child." Clay and Connie should be allowed to talk about Trent just like other parents talk about their children. Trent is just as real as any other child. The only difference is that he is not here anymore.

Not everyone who has experienced loss is as comfortable talking about their deceased loved one as Clay and I are. It is perfectly valid and healthy for these people to not share Clay's and my enthusiasm in talking about those whom they have lost.

A friend of ours recently lost her husband suddenly and unexpectedly. I asked her if she is comfortable when people bring up her late husband in conversation and share their memories of him. Her answer: "It depends." She said that sometimes it is simply too painful, and she prefers for people not to bring him up. At other times, she is able to talk about him without breaking down, and she does not mind people bringing him up. It just depends on how she is doing emotionally at that moment.

Another dear friend recently revealed to me that, many years ago, he and his wife lost their only son and both of his wife's parents in a tragic automobile accident. My friend became emotional as he recounted the details of that horrible day long ago. It was still vividly fresh in his memory all these years later. He has not told many people about his loss. His wife does not like to talk about it at all and has felt that way ever since their loss. He said it is just too painful for her. She has found other ways of dealing with her heartache through the years. She has lived a productive life, so I would not say that it has been unhealthy for her to not talk about her loss. Each person grieves in their own way. Talking about her loss has not been one of the ways that she has chosen to deal with her grief, and that is okay.

So, how do you know if a particular person is comfortable talking about their loss? How do you know if it will bring encouragement or discouragement to them by talking about their loved one? The simplest way that I know of is to just ask them.

Wisdom and Love

As I mentioned earlier, no one said that grief was going to be easy. The same is true of helping a friend or loved one who is grieving. There is no instruction manual that spells out, step by step, exactly what you are supposed to do and say at each stage in your friend's grief journey that will be the most helpful to them. In fact, no such instruction manual would even be possible, due to the principles of grief that we have already discussed.

> There is no such thing as a pre-defined "grieving process." There is no universal, one-size-fits-all formula for grieving or grief management. No two people grieve in exactly the same way.

Because your friend is unique, and his or her situation is unique; because your relationship with your friend is unique, it is up to you to figure out the best way to be of help. As you consider the suggestions made in this chapter and in other places throughout this book, there are two guiding principles that will help you be a source of strength and encouragement to your grieving friend.

Ask God for Wisdom

"If any of you lacks wisdom, he should ask God, who gives generously to all without finding fault, and it will be given to him" (James 1:5 NIV). Any time a Christian is faced with a dilemma in which wisdom is needed to make the right decision, God has promised to provide such wisdom to the believer who does not doubt.

What a beautiful promise to the person who so desperately wants to help a grieving friend. When you don't know what to say or do; when you are afraid of saying or doing the wrong thing; when more than anything else you just want to hold your friend's broken heart in your loving hands and provide comfort and peace, but you are not sure exactly how to do that; God steps in and says, "Just ask me. I'll help you figure out how to help your friend."

Love is the Main Thing

Helping a grieving friend is more of a heart thing than a head thing. Don't spend a lot of time trying to figure out the logical thing to say or do. Grief has very little to do with logic.

After praying for God to give you wisdom, the best thing you can do is to simply love. Whatever words you speak, whatever actions you pursue, just let your heart be your guide. Act and speak out of unselfish love for your friend, and you will be a blessing to his or her broken heart.

God bless you as you strive to bless those who are grieving.

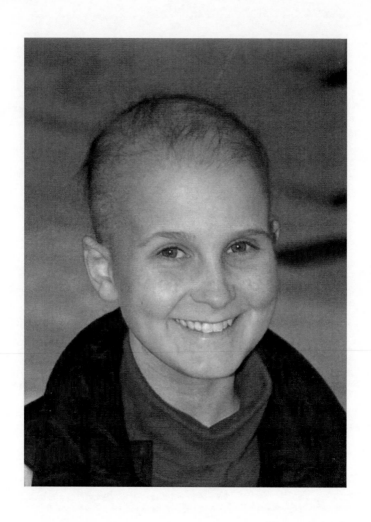

Choose to be Happy

During the time that Ashley was battling cancer, I wrote a series of articles for our local newspaper. One of those articles was entitled, "Choose to be Happy," and is reprinted below. It appeared in the Waxahachie Daily Light on Thursday, June 16, 1997.

Choose to be Happy

"Those who wish to sing always find a song."

I'm not sure who wrote those words, but I like the thought they express. I tend to believe that life is what we make of it, that "destiny is not a matter of chance; it is a matter of choice," and that our circumstances can only control us if we allow them to. And so, I believe with every fiber of my being that happiness is a choice. That's right, you can be happy simply by choosing to be happy. It doesn't matter how deep in debt you are; it doesn't matter how many health problems you have or how serious they are; it doesn't matter what your mother-in-law is like; it just doesn't matter—period! You can be happy simply by choosing to be happy.

I have philosophically accepted this idea for a long time, but let me tell you how I have recently become absolutely convinced of its undeniable truth. Just over three months ago, my wife and I sat outside the CAT scan room at Children's Medical Center in Dallas at 2:30 on a Sunday morning, and listened with disbelief as a doctor told us that our nine-year-old daughter Ashley had a brain tumor. The sense of shock and horror and numbness and denial that hit us like a ton of bricks when we heard those words, simply defies adequate description. I remember hearing Susan say several times during those first few days, "it's like this is all just a bad dream." The only problem was, we weren't waking up.

In the short time that it took the doctor to utter those words, "Your daughter has a brain tumor," our world was completely, instantly, irreversibly turned upside down. The next few weeks were filled with tests, surgeries, doctors, nurses, medicines, and lots of nights spent sleeping—or trying to sleep—in uncomfortable positions in hospital rooms, with all sorts of gadgets hanging off of the walls and rolling around beeping on poles with wheels. For six weeks, we drove to Dallas every weekday for Ashley to receive radiation treatment. After each of her first two treatments, she became violently ill in reaction to the radiation. We were helpless. We had to just sit there and watch as her body convulsed mercilessly. We wiped her forehead in-between heaves for the duration of the two-hour-long episodes. Finally, her extreme nausea and vomiting were controlled with a relatively new, and quite expensive, drug.

Then her hair fell out. Susan and the kids had traveled down to the Austin area for the weekend to visit grandmothers. A dear friend, who had been Ashley's first grade teacher in Georgetown, French-braided Ashley's hair. The next night, back at home in Waxahachie, Ashley asked Susan to take her hair down because the braids were bothering her. As Susan worked the braids loose, Ashley's hair began coming out in huge clumps. By the time Susan was through, Ashley had almost no hair left on her head. She was devastated. She went back into her room and cried. I walked back there, my heart aching unbearably. I couldn't think of a word to say that would ease her pain, so I just sat there gently stroking her.

She learned to deal quite remarkably with the hair loss and with the patch that she still wears over one eye because of the double vision that has troubled her for three months now. She handled the remainder of her radiation treatments beautifully. She is at summer camp this week, and then goes back into the hospital next week to begin the next phase of treatment, where her body will begin to be introduced to four different very powerful chemotherapy drugs that will hopefully kill any remaining cancer cells over the next year. The only bad thing is that these drugs also have the potential to cause some rather serious side effects.

So why am I telling you all this? Let me try to explain. I am not seeking your pity. I don't want people feeling sorry for us. Our lives are blessed in so many ways. We have so much for which to be thankful. There is much joy and laughter in our lives. Yes, you read that correctly. We laugh a lot. We are happy! Hey, that reminds me of what I was talking about at first! You see, we are faced with a set of circumstances that we would not have chosen if we had been given the option. But we weren't given the option. The circumstances are here, so we have to deal with them. There are certain options that we do have, however.

Ashley has cancer. We can be miserable and walk around with a poor-pitiful-us-look-at-what-we-have-to-go-through attitude, or we can be happy and decide to go ahead and laugh and have fun anyway. We simply choose to be happy and laugh and have fun. Did that make the cancer go away? Nope. Did that keep her hair from falling out? Nope. Did that cause her vision to return to normal? Nope. But I'll tell you what our decision does do. It makes the cancer, and the hair loss, and the double vision, and this whole big mess that we are having to go through...a whole lot easier to go through.

Now I'm gonna get religious on you for just a minute (sorry, it's an occupational hazard!). God never promised us that life would be peachy keen and trouble-free if we followed him. What he did promise us, in Romans 8:28, is that he could take anything that happens to us, good or bad, and make good stuff come from it. Is Ashley's cancer a good thing? Nope. Can something good come from it? You better believe it! And we have already seen that happen.

So, it's your choice. Problems are going to come around and visit you. That's a given. The money will run out before the month does. You will get sick. If you get married, you will have a mother-in-law— by the way, just in case anyone is wondering, I have a wonderful mother-in-law! The cat will have fleas, the baby will puke all over your best Sunday clothes, your brand new car will get a ding or scratch right where everyone will see it. And someone you love will probably get cancer. And even when all of those things happen on the same day, you can be happy if you want to be. It's that simple!

But What About Depression?

I want to be happy. I've tried the whole choosing to be happy thing. I've given myself pep talks. I've tried thinking happy thoughts. I've tried finding my "happy place." I've tried listening to happy music. Nothing works. Why can't I be happy? What's wrong with me?

First of all, you are not alone. While I firmly believe the general principle that "happiness is a choice" as expressed above, I have also come to know that for some people, it just isn't that simple. Many people struggle daily trying to achieve even a small degree of happiness, to no avail. To them, happiness is elusive; it is always just out of reach. They cannot explain it, and they do not completely understand it. All they know is that they just cannot seem to find happiness. There always seems to be a dark cloud of despair and depression hanging over their heads, and they do not know how to get out from under it.

"Depression" used to be an ugly word. It was one of those things you did not talk about openly because it carried a stigma of weakness, or it meant you had "issues" or were emotionally unstable.

"When you have depression, it's more than feeling sad. Intense feelings of sadness and other symptoms, like losing interest in things you enjoy, may last for a while. Depression is a medical illness, not a sign of weakness. And it's treatable".[1]

Doctors and researchers have long believed that depression is caused by a chemical imbalance in the brain.[2] This means that it is physiological, not just "mental."

"Brain-imaging technologies, such as magnetic resonance imaging (MRI), have shown that the brains of people who have depression look different than those of people without depression. The parts of the brain involved in mood, thinking, sleep, appetite, and behavior appear different".[3]

In February 2012 I developed a sore on the bottom of my left foot that became severely infected. On the day that I was to go see my family doctor, I woke up with a fever in excess of 104 degrees Fahrenheit. For about two or three hours straight, I experienced uncontrollable shaking. I was so weak by the time I got to the doctor's office that I could barely stand up straight. The doctor examined me and immediately sent me across the street to the hospital. Late that night, I was taken to the operating room where the wound on my foot was surgically debrided and drained of infectious fluids.

Cultures taken from the wound on my foot revealed that I had developed a staph infection in the wound. Blood cultures showed that the infection had made its way into my bloodstream and had begun spreading throughout my body. It was this rapidly spreading staph infection that had caused my high fever, uncontrollable shaking, and other physiological symptoms. I remained in the hospital for an entire week being treated with intravenous antibiotics. I was released from the hospital with a PICC line[4] in my right arm so that I could continue receiving IV antibiotics for an additional six weeks at home. In summary, my body was not functioning normally, so I required medical treatment to return my body to its normal function.

Depression is very similar. It is not just a mental condition. It is not a sign that the depressed person is emotionally weak or unstable and just needs to "try harder" to be happy. The underlying cause of depression is physiological. There is a chemical imbalance in the brain. The good news is that it is treatable. Just like there were antibiotics that were available to treat and eradicate my staph infection, there are medications and other therapies that are available to treat depression.

Grief-Induced Depression

Intense, debilitating sadness is a natural component of grief. It is completely normal for sadness to be the dominant emotional characteristic of your life immediately following the death of a loved one. As we have discussed at length, there is no magic formula for overcoming grief. There is no universal timetable that can tell you when you should expect to quit being sad and start being happy again.

Actually, I don't think that's even a realistic expectation. I do not expect to ever completely quit being sad, because my heart will always be broken over the loss of my precious Ashley. But here's the thing. My heart doesn't have to quit being sad in order for me to once again experience happiness. I firmly believe that grief and happiness can peacefully co-exist.

Sadness will always be present in my heart. It will not always be prominent, but it will always be there to some degree. Joy has always been the defining characteristic of my life. Grief did not change that. It did not steal my joy from me. It simply moved it, temporarily, to a place of lesser prominence. When Ashley died, sadness became the dominant emotion in my heart. Eventually, however, I regained a healthy balance between sadness and joy.

If you feel that you are having difficulty re-establishing that healthy balance; if it seems that sadness is sticking around too long as the dominant emotion of your heart and you do not seem to be able to reconnect with the joy that once defined you, then you may be experiencing depression. Visit with your doctor and express your concerns.

Depression is not hopeless, and it does not have to be permanent. There are treatments available. You can once again experience happiness and joy. Don't give up!

The God Factor

Why?

I have spent nearly my entire adult life as a minister, trying to help people connect with God. When that connection is broken, I try to help people find their way back to God.

I believe from the very deepest place in my soul that God is real, and that he genuinely loves us and is concerned about us. I also believe that God is all-powerful and can heal any disease of the body, mind, or soul with no difficulty whatsoever. I believe God could have taken away Ashley's cancer in the blink of an eye. I fervently pleaded with him, over and over, to do just that. In fact, thousands of people all over the world asked him to take Ashley's cancer away. So why didn't he?

I don't know the answer to that question and probably never will. I could allow that unanswered question to gradually eat away at my soul, creating an increasing level of doubt, and eventually destroying my trust in God. If I choose that path, obviously my faith cannot survive. So, choosing to linger on the question *why* has the potential to completely destroy my faith.

On the other hand, I can simply choose to accept God's wisdom and authority and not pursue an answer to the question *why*. For many people, that is a difficult choice to make. As human beings, we have an inherent need to understand the reasons why things happen, especially in a situation as life-changing and as completely unfair and senseless as losing a child to a deadly disease. The problem is, there is probably no answer that would even come anywhere close to being satisfactory.

"Why did God allow Ashley to die at age fourteen instead of healing her of cancer, as so many thousands of people persistently asked Him to do?" Let's explore a couple of possible answers to that question.

Possible Answer Number One

"God needed another angel."

Seriously? I could easily and very convincingly argue that my need for Ashley to stay here and continue living and grow up and get married and give me grandchildren ... was much greater than God's need for Ashley to come to heaven and be an angel among the already innumerable host of angels. (I'm not sure about the theology behind that whole scenario anyway, that people who die become angels.)

I could easily and very convincingly argue that Susan's need for her only daughter to remain alive and continue to bless her with all the beauty of the mother-daughter relationship was much greater than God's need for another angel.

I could easily and very convincingly argue that Justin's need to have his big sister here to love him through all the relationship challenges and just plain stupidity that junior high, high school and college would foist upon him was much greater than God's need for another angel. There have been many times when he *needed* his big sister, and she was not here, and his broken heart was trampled all over again as a result.

I'm sorry, but the "God needed another angel" theory, as cute and fluffy as it sounds, just does not hold water; and in fact is kind of like a slap in the face.

Possible Answer Number Two

"God knew that Ashley's life would be filled with pain and suffering if she remained here, so he mercifully chose to remove her from that pain and suffering."

Sorry, that one doesn't work either, because it assumes that God's only option for saving Ashley from pain and suffering was to take her to heaven. God, being all-powerful, could have easily taken away the pain and suffering and left her here, instead of taking her away from here in order to prevent further pain and suffering. Remember, we're talking about an all-powerful God here, not a God whose powers are limited. Let's be careful not to place restrictions on God in our attempt to come up with palatable answers to the question, "Why?"

The bottom line is this. I will never know exactly why God chose to answer my prayer, "No." And make no mistake about it; his answer was clearly "No." I prayed and prayed for God to physically heal Ashley of cancer. I specifically begged him to remove her tumor and completely restore her health. I did not leave any "wiggle room" that would allow me to explain it away if it didn't turn out the way I wanted it to. I was very specific in my request. And I was not the only one praying.

There were literally thousands of people all over the world who were fervently taking Ashley's name to God in prayer, asking him to provide the same healing for which I pleaded. There is no way around it. God clearly chose to answer all of those prayers ... "No."

Uncomfortable Principles

As frustrating as it may be to realize that I will never know for certain why that was God's answer, there are some principles that can help me understand Ashley's death—and God's choice to allow her to die—from a little different perspective. These principles can also help the grieving soul find some sense of peace in the midst of turmoil. They are uncomfortable principles, perhaps kind of hard to swallow. But they are real. And they are biblical.

I once heard someone say, "God is not as concerned with your comfort as he is with your character." Sometimes we want God to step in and fix everything that is broken in our lives so that we do not have to suffer anymore. Does he have the power to do that? Absolutely. So why wouldn't he?

Do you remember the apostle Paul's "thorn in the flesh"?

> To keep me from becoming conceited because of these surpassingly great revelations, there

was given me a thorn in my flesh, a messenger
of Satan, to torment me. Three times I pleaded
with the Lord to take it away from me. But
he said to me, "My grace is sufficient for you,
for my power is made perfect in weakness."
Therefore I will boast all the more gladly about
my weaknesses, so that Christ's power may
rest on me. That is why, for Christ's sake, I
delight in weaknesses, in insults, in hardships,
in persecutions, in difficulties. For when I am
weak, then I am strong.

(2 Corinthians 12:7–10 NIV)

No one knows exactly what Paul's thorn in the
flesh was, but many scholars believe it was some
form of physical infirmity or disability. It was clearly
something that Paul would rather have lived without.
He described it as "a messenger of Satan, to torment
me." Whatever it was, it caused Paul a great deal of
frustration and maybe even pain. He asked God to take
it away. He didn't just ask once, he didn't just ask twice.
Three times Paul pleaded with God to take away his
infirmity. God's answer? "No."

Sometimes God can accomplish more through our
sufferings than he can through our strengths.

We have already seen the promise in Romans 8:28
that all things work together for good in the lives
of those who love him. God can take even our most
difficult circumstances and turn them around to result
in good things happening in our lives and/or the lives
of others. God told Paul, "My power is made perfect in

weakness." Paul realized that, with God's grace to see him through, "when I am weak, then I am strong."

Welcome to Walmart!

To help us better understand this idea that good things can come out of difficult circumstances, and that God can accomplish more through our sufferings than he can through our strengths, let's look at the lives of two men and compare them, side by side.

First, there's Fred. Fred has been a "brittle diabetic" since he was a teenager. When he was 35, he had his right leg amputated because of diabetic foot ulcers that became irreversibly infected. At age 38, his left leg was amputated. Fred was now confined to a wheelchair and could no longer perform the tasks that his factory job required him to do. After 20 years of service, his employer had to lay him off. Fred was devastated.

He immediately started looking for work, and got a job as a Walmart greeter. Because of the reduction in salary, Fred lost his four-bedroom house and moved his family into a two-bedroom apartment.

These are certainly not pleasant circumstances, but Fred shows up at Walmart 20 minutes early every day and greets every customer who comes through the doors with a huge smile and a genuine "God bless you!"

Fred is the first one to volunteer almost any time something needs to be done at church that he is capable of doing. Because he enjoys greeting people at Walmart, he volunteered to serve as a greeter at church, too. He makes sure he is there early every Sunday, parks his wheelchair right in the middle of the main entrance, and greets everyone who walks through the doors with a handshake or hug, a huge smile, and a heartfelt, "God bless you! It's so good to see you today!"

The other fellow we will look at is George. George has never been sick a day in his life. His father is a high-ranking government official, so George's family has never hurt for money. When George was twenty-two years old, his dad pulled a few strings and got him a cushy job at an investment firm. George did quite well at his job, pulling in a very respectable salary. He married his college sweetheart and they purchased a lavish house in a high-end gated community. When children came along and grew to be school-age, George enrolled them in the finest private school he could find.

George and his family are members of the same church as Fred and his family. Every Sunday when George walks through the church's front doors, he is greeted with an enthusiastic handshake and smile from Fred, and a heartfelt, "God bless you, George! It's so good to see you today!"

Let me ask you a question. Whose life exhibits a more powerful testimony of faith? The obvious answer is Fred. Does that mean George is a bad person? Not at all! George also volunteers for numerous tasks at church, serves as a deacon, gives generously to the church in the weekly contribution, participates wholeheartedly in Bible classes, and strives diligently to be the spiritual leader that his wife and kids need him to be. George is a good man, and has his own testimony of faith.

But Fred's testimony is more powerful and connects with more people because he has held onto his faith, and even grown in his faith, in spite of difficult circumstances. He is always cheerful and is always encouraging other people. The circumstances of Fred's life could have destroyed his faith, but Fred simply chose to trust in God and take him at his word, believing that God would take Fred's difficult circumstances and make something good come from them. Because of Fred's upbeat attitude, his spirit of encouragement, and his unwavering faith, he is an inspiration to all who know him. God is using Fred's life, despite his difficulties (or maybe even as a result of his difficulties?) to bless many other people's lives.

That is exactly what Ashley's life was like. Her courage and determination and unwavering faith in the midst of insurmountable obstacles inspired thousands of people all over the world. So, if God's answer to my prayers for Ashley's healing was something like this— "Paul, I know your heart is breaking over Ashley's suffering, but because of her faithful spirit I can use her to touch more people's lives through her suffering than I can by healing her"—that certainly does not lessen the pain of watching her suffer, but it does at least put it in perspective—an eternal perspective—and makes me grateful that I was blessed to witness such a remarkable life.

Here's the one that's even tougher to swallow. If God's answer to my prayer for Ashley's life to be spared was something like this—"Paul, I know how much this is going to break your heart; I, too, had to watch my child suffer mercilessly and die, so I know the unfathomable pain you are about to experience; but bringing Ashley home to heaven now will exponentially increase the power of her faithful testimony while she was alive, much more than if I were to allow her to remain with you"—that certainly does not ease the pain in my forever-broken heart, but it does give me a different perspective—an eternal perspective—on the whole thing.

And since I'm imagining what God might have been saying to me through Ashley's sickness and death, let me speculate one step further. I can feel God's powerfully gentle hand on my shoulder as he reassures me. "Don't worry about Ashley. She's okay. I am taking good care of her. I know your heart is broken beyond repair, but I will help you wade through all of that pain and make some sense of it all. I am here with you, Paul. And don't forget, Ashley has reached her goal! Someday, I will welcome you to this magnificent place as I have already welcomed her and your precious dad. That will be a glorious day, Paul; I can promise you that! Just don't give up. Just keep letting your faith shine through like Ashley did, and everything will turn out okay. And remember, I am with you always."

God of the Brokenhearted

All throughout this book, one of my basic underlying premises that provides the foundation for my philosophy of grief is, "Hearts broken by grief cannot be fixed." In the context of this chapter, "The God Factor," that basic premise begs the question, "But can't *God* fix a heart that is broken by grief?"

The easy answer is yes. God is all-powerful, so certainly he has the power to fix or heal a broken heart. Then why doesn't he?

From my observations, I think it is safe to say that every person I can think of who has ever lost someone whom they dearly loved has experienced a perpetually broken heart. It seems to be a reality, then, that even though God has the power to completely eradicate the pain of grief from broken hearts, he consistently chooses not to do so.

I cannot pretend to know what God's reasons are, "'For my thoughts are not your thoughts, neither are your ways my ways,' declares the Lord" (Isaiah 55:8 NIV). I do, however, understand that a broken heart can actually be useful. Perhaps that is one reason why God allows broken hearts to remain broken.

My broken heart is useful because it reminds me how special Ashley was. Ashley was my firstborn child and my only daughter. She brought an abundance of joy into my life when she was born. She opened up a whole new world of experience for Susan and me, as young parents, which we would never have known had we not become parents. She was bright, and a little bit mischievous, constantly keeping me on my toes to try and stay one step ahead of her. She gave the best hugs! Her courage and determination and faith in the face of cancer inspired me and taught me and sharpened my own faith. Her compassion for others, her love of little children, that smile of hers that came from deep within her soul—all of these things caused me often to step back and just say, "Wow! What an incredible kid. I want to be like her!"

I could fill volumes describing all the things that made Ashley special, and all the things I miss about her because she is gone. What would it say about her—and about my relationship with her—if that hole in my heart could be filled, if that nagging emptiness were able to just go away, if one day the pain caused by her absence just completely vanished? Her absence hurts so much because her presence brought so much joy. I do not want my broken heart to ever be "fixed." I do not want the pain and emptiness of missing her to ever completely go away, because they are powerful reminders of just how special Ashley was.

My broken heart is useful because it makes heaven seem that much more real. I have always believed in the reality of heaven, that it is an actual place, a spiritual paradise reserved for those who choose to faithfully serve God while here on earth. My faith assures me that Ashley is in heaven, along with my dad and my grandparents and other loved ones who have reached the end of their earthly journey. Knowing that she is there makes heaven even more real for me, and greatly increases my motivation to go there myself. I want to see Ashley again, and I firmly believe that we will be reunited someday. That anticipation fuels my desire to live faithfully, and the emptiness in my broken heart keeps that anticipation fresh every day.

My broken heart is useful because it allows me to help others who are hurting. There have been several times when someone has approached me or Susan to tell us about another family who has lost a child, and to ask if we would be willing to talk to them. My answer has always been yes, *if* the other family actually wants to talk. I do not presume to know exactly what they are going through because every person's grief journey is unique. I do not usually have a lot of wisdom or sage advice, because that is usually not what the other family is looking for. However, because my heart is also broken, that provides a point of connection that allows me to have a certain level of understanding of where they are. It gives them a sense that I am someone with whom they can connect. Often they are not looking for advice or answers; they are simply looking for a shoulder to cry on, for someone who will listen, for someone who simply understands. I can provide that, because I have been where they are.

The Psalmist said, "The Lord is near to those who have a broken heart" (Psalm 34:18 NIV). God's answer is not always "yes," but it is always the right answer.

"Until Then" recording session.
Top photo: Paul and Justin O'Rear.
Bottom photo: Justin O'Rear and Jeremy Pate.

Until Then

Tennessee

Ashley died in November 2001. We planned a trip to Tennessee the following March, during Justin's Spring Break, to visit some dear friends—Don and Debbie Dabbs—and to spend a few days in the Great Smoky Mountains.

The week before we were to leave, we learned that one of Ashley's "cancer buddies," Lea Clancy, had passed away. Lea was ten years old and had been battling cancer for five and a half years. She was a precious little girl. Our families had become close through our shared cancer experience. We had run into each other numerous times through the years at various events hosted by Children's Medical Center for their cancer patients. When we learned of Lea's death, our hearts broke for Steve and Cyndi and their family as they began their long journey of grief, learning how to live without Lea. We attended Lea's funeral on Saturday, then headed for Tennessee.

Several weeks earlier some thoughts had started tumbling around in my head for a song in Ashley's memory. I did not write any of it down at the time, but the words "until then" kept surfacing. In my mind I was picturing different phases of Ashley's life, and during each of those phases there was something we were looking forward to. Even in her death, we had the sweet anticipation of a heavenly reunion. "Until then" was becoming the hook around which the rest of the song would build itself.

On the trip to Tennessee, all those ideas started running through my mind again. They began taking shape as a tribute to the remarkable life of my Ashley, her profound impact on our lives, and the deep emptiness left in our hearts by her death. Even amid the deep sadness of our grief, though, I found my thoughts, and the emerging song, focusing on the hope that is inherent in our faith—the promise that, one day, we will see her and hold her once again.

It was the middle of the night. We were on a long, lonely stretch of highway somewhere between Texas and Tennessee. My mind was racing with all these thoughts and ideas for a song. As the thoughts and ideas began to organize themselves into specific verses and a chorus, I asked Susan to find a pen and some paper and start writing down the words as they came to me. I drove and she wrote and by the time we reached Tennessee, "Until Then" was a song.

The next morning we stopped at an electronics store and purchased a microcassette recorder. Sitting in the car outside the electronics store, I made a very rough recording of myself singing the song. The words were all on paper, but I did not want to lose the tune that I had come up with the night before to fit the words.

Later that day we arrived at Don and Debbie's house outside of Nashville. Don and Debbie had become cherished friends over the years. We initially met them through a business venture that we were both involved in. Our friendship was almost instant. They are the kind of people who, five minutes after we met, we felt like we had known them our entire lives. When Don and Debbie moved from Texas to Tennessee, we kept in touch with them. Several times through the years we found reasons to travel to Tennessee so that we could see them.

This particular trip was intended to be an opportunity to get away as a family and spend some time healing. I have always loved Tennessee, especially the Great Smoky Mountains. The seemingly untouched beauty of nature that is found throughout the park—the huge trees, the beautiful mountains that seem so surreal when enveloped in the early morning bluish fog that casts an eerie haze over the entire area, the amazing variety of bird and animal life, and the temporary slower pace of life created by such serene environs— connects with my soul in a way that few places on earth do. Tennessee is therapeutic for me, and we were needing something therapeutic.

While we were at Don and Debbie's house, I played my rough recording of "Until Then" for Don. He really liked it. As soon as it had finished playing, Don asked me a question that caught me completely off guard. "Who do you envision singing your song?" After I replayed that question over in my mind a couple of times, I realized that Don was asking me if I had thought of trying to get a professional, popular singer to record my song. Maybe it seemed like a natural question to Don, simply because he lived in the Country Music capital of the world; but I had not even contemplated such a possibility at this point in the game! It did, however, plant a seed of thought in my mind. I found myself wondering, "Is this song actually good enough to someday be recorded by a professional singer?" It was an exciting proposition, and I could not get Don's question out of my mind.

Karen and Karen

Before we left Nashville and headed east to the Smokies, we had the privilege of meeting up with two other very special people. "Aunt Karen" had been one of Ashley's nurses during those long days and weeks at Children's Medical Center. We had developed a deep appreciation for nurses throughout Ashley's cancer ordeal, and there were several who rose to the top of the pack as some of our favorites. Karen was in that upper echelon. She loved Ashley dearly, and always treated Ashley—and our whole family—with tender loving care. She was so special that Ashley started calling her "Aunt Karen."

I knew that Karen had moved to the Nashville area when she left Dallas. With Don's help and a quick e-mail consultation with another of our favorite nurses back in Dallas, we were able to locate Karen in the phone book. I called her, and the next evening we all met for dinner at a local restaurant. We had a wonderful time catching up on old times. Seeing Karen again was a serendipitous treat for my family, and considerably increased the therapeutic value of the trip.

I introduced you to another Karen earlier in the book, in the chapter entitled "Grieve in Your Own Way." Karen Taylor-Good is an accomplished singer-songwriter from Nashville who lost her nephew Paul when he was twenty-one years old. She wrote the song "Precious Child" in his honor. We played that song at Ashley's funeral, and it became a song of special significance to our family, especially to Justin.

I sent an e-mail to Karen shortly after Ashley's death to let her know that we had played "Precious Child" at the funeral. She sent back a very gracious reply. As the Tennessee trip neared, I contacted Karen again to let her know that we were going to be in Nashville for a couple of days and would love to meet her if that was possible. Through a series of e-mails, a meeting was arranged. She met us at a nearby Cracker Barrel restaurant and we had a very enjoyable visit. She is a lovely, warm, genuinely caring person.

Near the end of our visit I played my rough recording of "Until Then" for Karen. She was very kind in her comments about my song. I asked her what it would take to obtain a professionally-recorded instrumental track to go behind the lyrics. She said that she would check around with some of her Nashville musician friends and get back to me. A couple of weeks later I received an e-mail from Karen with the contact information for some studio musicians who had agreed to record a guitar track for the song at a greatly-reduced fee. Even though it was a phenomenal offer, I did not have the money; so I never pursued that route. I felt bad (and still do) because Karen had gone to bat for me and I had dropped the ball.

I have been in contact with Karen several times since then, and she has never been anything but kind and loving in our exchanges. She has never expressed any disappointment with me for not following up on the information she provided me. I am indebted to her for her continued kindness.

Karen Taylor-Good (center) with
Justin and Susan O'Rear

A Fascinating Journey

Over the next several months, I continued to share "Until Then" with a few people here and there, and was always pleased with the feedback I received. Jeremy Pate, a dear friend and fellow youth minister, heard the song and offered to record an instrumental track to go behind the lyrics. He and his cousin Steve Agee proceeded to do just that. The end result was a wonderful instrumental track featuring guitar and drums.

Another good friend, Randy McCoy, was running a professional recording studio in Fort Worth at the time. I shared with him my dream of getting a good recording of "Until Then" using the instrumental track provided by Jeremy and Steve. Randy offered to help.

On Thursday evening, December 2, 2004, I met Randy at the recording studio. Jeremy and my son Justin were with me. The first step was to record my vocals on top of the instrumental track, often re-recording a single phrase several times to get it just right. It was a fascinating and tedious process.

After the lead vocals were recorded, Jeremy and Justin each took their turn at the microphone, Jeremy singing high harmonies and Justin singing low harmonies. It took two sessions to finish recording all the parts and get everything just right. Randy was very picky throughout the entire recording process, a trait I came to appreciate after I heard the finished recording. I was very pleased with the final sound.

To have Jeremy help with the vocals, after having already contributed enormously to the project by providing the instrumental track, was very special. To have Justin be such an integral part of this project commemorating the life of his beloved big sister was meaningful beyond description.

I wanted to put together a fully-packaged CD of the song, so that I could share it with friends and family as a finished product. The next step was to create the

CD packaging. For the front cover graphic, I turned once again to my buddy Jeremy. Not only is he gifted musically, he is even more gifted in the field of graphic art and design. He agreed to help me.

I had a couple of vague ideas that I pitched to Jeremy. On the last Father's Day card I received from Ashley, she had drawn a uniquely shaped heart that really caught my attention. I asked Jeremy to incorporate that heart into the front cover design somehow.

One of my all-time favorite photos of Ashley is a picture that came to be known as "the purple sunglasses picture." Sometime in the fall of 1996, a few months before she was diagnosed with cancer, Ashley had gone over to her friend Jessica's house to play. When I went to pick her up, Ashley was wearing a pair of Jessica's overalls and some purple sunglasses. Purple was absolutely her favorite color. I asked her to sit down in a chair on Jessica's back porch so that I could take a quick picture. I snapped several pictures and then we got in the car and left. When the pictures came back from the photo lab, there was one photo in particular that jumped out and grabbed me.

Ashley was adorably cute to begin with, mostly because I married well. In this particular photo, her beautiful "dirty blonde" hair fell perfectly on her shoulders. She had the purple sunglasses perched on the end of her cute little pug nose, so that her hazel eyes were peering over the top of the sunglasses, looking right into the camera. She was smiling, not a huge cheesy smile but kind of a contented, relaxed smile. The purple lenses of the sunglasses and the deep denim blue of the overalls complemented each other beautifully. Every element of the photo came together perfectly. I asked Jeremy to incorporate this photo into the CD cover art as well.

The design that Jeremy put together was brilliant. The heart shape covered almost the entire CD cover. He created a pencil sketch of the purple sunglasses picture and put it inside the heart. Then he hand-colored the sunglasses lenses purple, so that they popped against the black-and-white of the sketch.

I took Jeremy's design to another graphic artist friend, Andy Moya, and asked him if he would create a unified packaging design that incorporated Jeremy's graphic. He agreed. Andy designed the front and back covers on a black background. He colored the heart shape a soft pink that blended beautifully with both the deep black background and the pencil sketch of Ashley.

Another of Ashley's signature photos is what I call the *headshot*. At one point during the in-between years—after her chemotherapy treatments had been completed and before she relapsed—Ashley decided that she wanted to try her hand at acting. We had received an advertising mailer from a Hollywood agency that had an office in Dallas, looking for potential child actors. Ashley was intrigued with the opportunity, so we set up an appointment for an interview. After sitting through the interview, Ashley was determined to pursue this opportunity.

We did not have the money to pay the hefty fee, but Ashley had enough money saved up and begged us to let her do it, so we did. The first order of business was to schedule a photo shoot with a professional photographer for the purpose of producing a headshot that the agency could use to promote Ashley as a child actor. We scheduled the photo shoot and ended up with several really good pictures, including the photo that the agency selected as her professional headshot.

Andy incorporated the headshot into the back cover of the CD, along with the song's lyrics and copyright information. I thought the overall packaging design was very attractive. I had a batch of CD jewel case inserts printed, using Jeremy and Andy's designs, and purchased a box of clear jewel cases. The project was coming together nicely.

In terms of the packaging, the only element left was the design on the CD itself. I used a black background in order to maintain consistency in the overall design. I used a photo of Ashley from the Olympic torch relay press conference at Dallas City Hall, with the photo positioned to the left of the CD's center hole. The title of the song across the top and a web address across the bottom completed the simple design.

Another very dear friend and fellow youth minister, Jon McKenzie, duplicated and printed the finished CD for me at cost. The end product was a professional-looking package that would have felt right at home in any music store's CD bins, and which I was proud to share with family and friends.

I am deeply indebted to all the people who helped me take this project from start to finish. The process of writing and recording the song, packaging the CD, and then personally distributing it to family and friends, was a deeply rewarding and personally gratifying experience. It is my sincere hope that other grievers who are so inclined will eagerly pursue the same goal and write a song in memory of their loved one.

My Dream

Ever since I wrote "Until Then," I have had a really big dream of someday having it recorded by a well-known country artist. At the time of this writing, I have no idea how to make that happen, but it continues to be a dream, for two reasons.

First, music is powerful and therapeutic. When Ashley was going through her cancer battle, and when she died, and even to this day, there have been a number of songs that have served as a source of strength for me and for my family. Music has the power to soothe the soul, to invoke reflection and soul-searching, and even to bring a sense of calm and peace. It is a crucial and fundamental element to life itself.

Knowing how therapeutic music has been for me, it is my hope that "Until Then" can provide that same sense of connection and healing for others who are traveling their own grief journey. Obviously, the more exposure the song gets, the better chance it has of helping other people. Having a well-known artist record the song would certainly get it in front of exponentially more people than I could ever hope to do on my own. So this is my altruistic reason for wanting to have "Until Then" recorded by a well-known artist. I want it to help people.

I also have a more selfish reason for wanting my song to reach lots of people. I desperately want to keep Ashley's memory alive. The following is an excerpt from a blog post I wrote in September 2008.

> For those families who are left with empty arms and broken hearts, one of their greatest fears is that the world will forget that their precious child was here. I know, because I am one of those brokenhearted daddies. There is a burning desire deep in my soul to keep Ashley's memory alive. I cannot explain it to those who have not walked my path. Nor will I apologize for it to those who do not understand. Ashley, quite simply, is worth remembering.

The more people who hear my song "Until Then," the more people will know about my Ashley. The more people who know about Ashley, the longer her memory will live on. The longer her memory lives on, the more people will be inspired to face their own struggles with the same courage, determination and faith that Ashley exhibited throughout her ordeal.

Until Then

©2002 Paul Harold O'Rear (BMI)

The day you came into my life, my world began anew.
I didn't know that love could run as deep as I love you.
Someday you will spread your wings and fly into the wind,
And I promise I will take good care of you … until then.

Until then, my arms will hold you each and every day.
Until then, we'll make some memories along the way.
Someday you will spread your wings and fly into the wind,
And I promise I will take good care of you … until then.

The day the doctors broke the news, my heart was torn in two.
I couldn't bear the thought of maybe one day losing you.
Every day I pray that you'll be healed and whole again,
And I'll be right here beside you all the way … until then.

Until then, my arms will hold you each and every day.
Until then, we'll fight for life, and hope, and hug, and pray.
Every day I pray that you'll be healed and whole again,
And I'll be right here beside you all the way … until then.

The day you went to heaven left a hole inside my heart,
And every day the emptiness reminds me we're apart.
One day I will see you and I'll hold you once again,
And I'll keep your love and laughter in my heart … until then.

Until then, my heart will hold you each and every day.
Until then, my memories of you will light my way.
One day I will see you and I'll hold you once again,
And I'll keep your love and laughter in my heart … until then.

And my memories of you will light my way … until then.

Eight Years Later

O n November 24, 2009, I wrote a letter to Ashley and posted it on my blog. It was the eighth anniversary of her death. I want to share it with you here because I think it captures the nature of a maturing grief—or at least of my maturing grief, realizing of course that no two grief journeys are exactly the same—and provides a meaningful perspective from down the road.

A Letter to Ashley

It's hard to believe it has been eight years: November 24, 2001. Sometimes it seems as though it was only yesterday that you left us, Ashley. Then there are moments when it seems that a lifetime has passed since that awful day.

I still miss you like crazy. We're doing okay, though. You taught us to cherish every day. Most days we remember to do that. You taught us to live life to the fullest, to squeeze every drop of adventure out of every day that God gives us. You showed us that the real beauty of life is living with a complete trust in God. It's funny how I've been a minister most of my adult life, but you figured that out so much better and lived it so much more completely than I ever have.

I'll never forget the words you told the TV reporters at the Olympic torch relay press conference in Dallas.

It was the same thing you told Kidd Kraddick when he called you really early that morning right before the Children's Cancer Fund Luncheon to interview you on KISS-FM. It was the same thing you told everyone just by the way you lived your life every single day. "Trust in God, and never give up." I've never seen that demonstrated so beautifully as I saw it in your life. Thank you for showing me what it's like to really, really trust in God, no matter what … and to never give up. I want to be like you, Ashley.

You would be so proud of Bubba. He is doing so well in college. He's studying to be an Ag Teacher. You're the one who started that, you know. When you first started raising pigs for 4H, he couldn't wait until he was old enough to raise pigs, too. And once he was old enough, you and he raised pigs together every year. Ag became such an important part of his life, in both 4H and FFA, that he decided he wants to be an Ag Teacher so he can help other kids experience all the same wonderful things that you and he experienced. And, do you know what I think? I think it's also one way that he stays connected to you. That's just my secret theory, but I think there's something to it.

Bubba still misses you, Sweetie Pie. You probably saw him carry your picture around on the front of his school binder, even in high school. You probably saw him and heard him those times that he went out to your grave to "see you" during his senior year. You probably know about the poems and stories he wrote about you after you died. You are part of his soul, Ashley, and you always will be. He has grown into a fine, strong, godly young man. I am so very blessed and so very proud to be his daddy, just like I am so very blessed and so very proud that I got to be your daddy.

And so, today, eight years since the last day I kissed your beautiful little bald head, we remember. We remember all the joy that you brought into our lives. We remember all the wonderful times we spent together. We are reminded how empty our lives are because you are not here, and yet how blessed our lives are because you are so very much still here. And our hearts ache, and our hearts laugh; and our eyes smile, and our eyes cry. And we remember.

Thank you, Ashley. Thank you for letting God touch the world through your beautiful smile and through your beautiful soul. Thank you for loving me and making it such a joy to be your daddy. Thank you for all the things you taught us about life, about courage, and about God. We will never forget.

And someday…someday…we will be together again. And I will hug you and never let go. And life will be perfect, forever.

Until then.

Appendix

Songs to Grieve By

Songs Played at Ashley's Funeral

"Ashokan Farewell"
Performed by Jay Ungar, Matt Glasser, Evan Stover,
Russ Barenburg and Molly Mason
Album: "The Civil War" (1990)

"Claudia's Theme"
Performed by Bruno Bertone Orchestra
Album: "Western Movie Themes" (1993)

"On My Way Home"
Performed by Enya
Album: "The Memory of Trees" (1995)

"It's So Hard To Say Goodbye To Yesterday"
Performed by Boyz II Men
Album: "Cooleyhighharmony" (1991)

"Say Goodnight"
Performed by Beth Nielsen Chapman
Album: "Sand and Water" (1997)

"Precious Child"
Performed by Karen Taylor-Good
Album: "On Angel's Wings" (2001)

NOTE: At the time of this writing, "Precious Child" is also available as a free MP3 download from Karen Taylor-Good's website, http://www.karentaylorgood. com.

A Cappella Songs Played at Ashley's Funeral

"He Knows"
Performed by Jerome Williams and Free Indeed
Album: "Sing A New Song: Volume Five" (1996)

"Peace"
Performed by Jerome Williams and Free Indeed
Album: "Sing A New Song: Volume Five" (1996)

"Hide Me Away, O Lord"
Performed by The Acappella Company
Album: "Acappella Praise & Worship: In God We Trust" (1995)

"God Bless You, Go With God"
Performed by His Image Singers
Album: "The Best of His Image Singers: Volume III" (1999)

"He is Wonderful"
Performed by Best Friends (from Lubbock Christian University)
Album: "We've Found a Place" (2001)

"The Greatest Commands"
Performed by Jerome Williams and Free Indeed
Album: "Sing A New Song: Volume Eight" (1999)

"You Are My All in All"
Performed by Jerome Williams and Free Indeed
Album: "Sing A New Song: Volume Seven" (1998)

"Create in Me a Clean Heart"
Performed by Jerome Williams and Free Indeed
Album: "Sing A New Song: Volume Seven" (1998)

"Day By Day"
Performed by Jerome Williams and Free Indeed
Album: "Sing A New Song: Volume Four" (1995)

"When the Night is Falling"
Performed by The Hallal Singers
Album: "The Singer's Worship Series 7: Sacrifice"

"Whispering Hope"
Performed by His Image Singers
Album: "The Best of His Image Singers: Volume III"
(1999)

Other Songs

"Finally Home"
Performed by MercyMe
Album: "All That Is Within Me" (2007)

"Sometimes When It Rains"
Performed by Secret Garden
Album: "Earthsongs" (2005)

"One More Day"
Performed by Diamond Rio
Album: "One More Day" (2001)

"Tears in Heaven"
Performed by Eric Clapton
Album: "Unplugged" (1992)

"No One Knows But You"
Performed by Beth Nielsen Chapman
Album: "Sand and Water" (1997)

"Over the Rainbow/Wonderful World"
Performed by Israel Kamakawiwo'ole
Album: "Facing Future" (1993)

"Holes In The Floor Of Heaven"
Performed by Steve Wariner
Album: "Burnin' the Roadhouse Down" (1998)

"Go Rest High On That Mountain"
Performed by Vince Gill
Album: "When Love Finds You" (1994)

"Lay Your Burden Down"
Performed by Chuck Girard
Album: "Chuck Girard" (1978)

"You Would Have Loved This"
Performed by Cori Connors
Album: "Sleepy Little Town" (2001)

"If I Had Only Known"
Performed by Reba McEntire
Album: "For My Broken Heart" (1991)

"You Can Let Go"
Performed by Crystal Shawanda
Album: "Dawn of a New Day" (2008)

"Fly"
Performed by Celine Dion
Album: "Falling Into You" (1996)

"My Heart Will Go On (Love Theme From 'Titanic')"
Performed by Celine Dion
Album: "Titanic" (1997)

"If I Could Be Where You Are"
Performed by Enya
Album: "Amarantine" (2005)

"I Miss My Friend"
Performed by Darryl Worley
Album: "I Miss My Friend" (2002)

"My Old Friend"
Performed by Tim McGraw
Album: "Live Like You Were Dying" (2004)

Other A Cappella Songs

"Go Rest High On That Mountain"
Performed by onevoice
Album: "Hope" (2000)

"Beautiful Isle"
Performed by onevoice
Album: "Hope" (2000)

"What a Day That Will Be"
Performed by onevoice
Album: "Hope" (2000)

"Heaven's Joy Awaits"
Performed by Doyle Lawson & Quicksilver
Album: "Heaven's Joy Awaits" (1993)

"We'll Soon Be Done With Troubles and Trials"
Performed by IIIrd Tyme Out
Album: "Singing On Streets Of Gold"

"It Is Well With My Soul"
Performed by True Lift
Album: "Wave of Grace: Hymns of Glory" (2005)

"Be With Me, Lord"
Performed by True Lift
Album: "Wave of Grace: Hymns of Comfort" (2005)

"Nearer, Still Nearer"
Performed by True Lift
Album: "Wave of Grace: Hymns of Comfort" (2005)

"I Need Thee Every Hour"
Performed by The Acappella Company
Album: "Acappella Praise & Worship: Acappella Praise
Service" (1996)

Notes

An Angel Gets Her Wings

1. American Brain Tumor Association, *A Primer of Brain Tumors: A Patient's Reference Manual, Sixth Edition* (Chicago: American Brain Tumor Association, n.d.), 44.

2. Ibid.

3. Wikipedia contributors, "Port (medical)," *Wikipedia, The Free Encyclopedia* (San Francisco: Wikimedia Foundation, Inc., October 1, 2013), http://en.wikipedia.org/w/index.php?title=Port_(medical)&oldid=575238885. A portacath "is a small medical appliance that is installed beneath the skin. A catheter connects the port to a vein. Under the skin, the port has a septum through which drugs can be injected and blood samples can be drawn many times, usually with less discomfort for the patient than a more typical 'needle stick'."

Other People's Expectations

1. Fern Hill, *Graduation to Glory* (Fort Worth: Star Bible Publications, Inc., 2000), Preface.

Grieve in Your Own Way

1. Larry Barber, *Love Never Dies: Embracing Grief with Hope and Promise* (Maitland, FL: Xulon Press, 2011), 54-60.

2. Ibid., back cover.

3. The Jester Co., Inc., "The Author: Biography of David Saltzman," *The Jester & Pharley Phund* (Palos Verdes Estates, CA: The Jester Co., Inc., 2010), http://www.thejester.org/author/.

4. The Jester Co., Inc., "TheJester.org: The home of 'The Jester Has Lost His Jingle' by David Saltzman," *The Jester & Pharley Phund* (Palos Verdes Estates, CA: The Jester Co., Inc., 2010), http://www.thejester.org/.

5. David Saltzman, *The Jester Has Lost His Jingle* (Palos Verdes Estates, CA: The Jester Co., Inc., 1995), book jacket.

6. John Wood, "Life and Other Lies–The Hope and Healing Project," *Kickstarter* (New York: Kickstarter, Inc., 2012), http://www.kickstarter.com/projects/1519551358/life-and-other-lies-the-hope-and-healing-project.

7. John Wood, *Life and Other Lies: Finding Meaning in Loss* (Charleston, SC: CreateSpace, 2011).

8. K T Good Music, "About Karen–Karen Taylor Good," *Karen Taylor Good—Official Website*

(Nashville: K T Good Music, 2012), http://www.karentaylorgood.com/about_karen.htm.

9. K T Good Music, "Free MP3 Downloads—Karen Taylor Good," *Karen Taylor Good—Official Website* (Nashville: K T Good Music, 2012), http://www.karentaylorgood.com/free_mp3_downloads.html.

10. Clayton Dabney Foundation for Kids with Cancer, "Clayton's Story," *Clayton Dabney Foundation for Kids* (Dallas: Clayton Dabney Foundation for Kids with Cancer, 2013), http://www.claytondabney.org/claytons_story.php.

11. Jeanne Prejean, "Clayton Dabney Foundation Benefits from Dale Hansen Going 'Unplugged'," *Sweet Charity* (Dallas: D Magazine Partners, Inc., 2009), http://sweetcharity.dmagazine.com/2009/10/01/clayton-dabney-foundation-benefits-from-dale-hansen-going-unplugged/.

12. Dabney Foundation, *Clayton's Story.*

13. Prejean, *Clayton Dabney Foundation.*

14. Clayton Dabney Foundation for Kids with Cancer, "Who We Are," *Clayton Dabney Foundation for Kids* (Dallas: Clayton Dabney Foundation for Kids with Cancer, 2013), http://www.claytondabney.org/who_are_we.php.

15. Podium Enterprises, "Welcome to Podium Enterprises," *Podium Enterprises: Nikki Stone* (Park City, UT: Podium Enterprises, 2008), http://www.nikkistone.com/.

16. Neal White, "A Real Hero," *Waxahachie Daily Light* (Waxahachie, TX: Waxahachie Daily Light, November 20, 2001).

17. The Gregg Pearson Foundation, "About the Gregg Pearson Foundation," *The Gregg Pearson Foundation, Inc.: Honoring Gregg by Helping Others* (Arlington, TX: The Gregg Pearson Foundation, 2012), http://www.greggpearson. org/about/.

18. The Gregg Pearson Foundation, "Gregg's Story," *The Gregg Pearson Foundation, Inc.: Honoring Gregg by Helping Others* (Arlington, TX: The Gregg Pearson Foundation, 2012), http://www. greggpearson.org/gregg/.

19. The Gregg Pearson Foundation, *The Gregg Pearson Foundation, Inc.: Honoring Gregg by Helping Others* (Arlington, TX: The Gregg Pearson Foundation, 2012), http://www. greggpearson.org/.

20. Rachel's Challenge, *Rachel's Challenge: Start a Chain Reaction* (Littleton, CO: Rachel's Challenge).

Look for the Good

1. United States Geological Survey, "Earthquake Details: Magnitude 9.1–OFF THE wEST COAST OF NORTHERN SUMATRA," *U.S. Geological Survey Home Page* (Reston, VA: U.S. Geological Survey, 2012), http://earthquake.

usgs.gov/earthquakes/eqinthenews/2004/us2004slav/us2004slav.php.

2. United States Geological Survey, "Earthquake Summary: Magnitude 9.1–OFF THE wEST COAST OF NORTHERN SUMATRA," *U.S. Geological Survey Home Page* (Reston, VA: U.S. Geological Survey, 2012), http://earthquake.usgs.gov/earthquakes/eqinthenews/2004/us2004slav/us2004slav.php#summary.

3. United States Geological Survey, "Earthquake Details: Magnitude 9.0–NEAR THE EAST COAST OF HONSHU, JAPAN," *U.S. Geological Survey Home Page* (Reston, VA: U.S. Geological Survey, 2012), http://earthquake.usgs.gov/earthquakes/recenteqsww/Quakes/usc0001xgp.php.

4. United States Geological Survey, "Earthquake Summary: Magnitude 9.0–NEAR THE EAST COAST OF HONSHU, JAPAN," *U.S. Geological Survey Home Page* (Reston, VA: U.S. Geological Survey, 2012), http://earthquake.usgs.gov/earthquakes/eqinthenews/2011/usc0001xgp/#summary.

5. Wikipedia contributors, "April 25–28, 2011 tornado outbreak," *Wikipedia, The Free Encyclopedia* (San Francisco: Wikimedia Foundation, Inc., February 19, 2012), http://en.wikipedia.org/w/index.php?title=April_25%E2%80%9328,_2011_tornado_outbreak&oldid=477748165.

6. Greg Forbes and Jonathan Erdman, "Tornado Outbreak: By the Numbers," *National and Local Weather Forecast, Hurricane, Radar and Report* (Atlanta: The Weather Channel, LLC, 2011), http://www.weather.com/outlook/weather-news/news/articles/tornado-outbreak-april2011-stats_2011-05-04.

7. National Weather Service, "April Severe Weather Events Set New Tornado Records for Alabama," *National Oceanic and Atmospheric Administration* (Birmingham: National Weather Service Weather Forecast Office, 2011), http://www.srh.noaa.gov/bmx/?n=climo_2011torstats.

8. Biography.com, "Steve Irwin," *The Biography Channel website* (New York: A&E Television Networks, LLC, n.d.), http://www.biography.com/people/steve-irwin-189158.

Choose to be Happy

1. WebMD, "Getting Help for Depression," *WebMD–Better information. Better health.* (Atlanta: WebMD, LLC, n.d.), http://www.webmd.com/depression/default.htm.

2. National Institute of Mental Health, "Depression," *National Institute of Mental Health (NIMH)* (Bethesda, MD: National Institute of Mental Health, 2011.), http://www.nimh.nih.gov/health/publications/depression/index.shtml.

3. Ibid.

4. Wikipedia contributors, "Peripherally inserted central catheter," *Wikipedia, The Free Encyclopedia*, (San Francisco: Wikimedia Foundation, Inc., October 2, 2013), http://en.wikipedia.org/w/index.php?title=Peripherally_inserted_central_catheter&oldid=575509663. "A peripherally inserted central catheter (PICC or PIC line) is a form of intravenous access that can be used for a prolonged period of time (e.g. for long chemotherapy regimens, extended antibiotic therapy, or total parenteral nutrition)...A PICC is inserted in a peripheral vein in the arm,...and then advanced through increasingly larger veins, toward the heart until the tip rests in the distal superior vena cava or cavoatrial junction."